A
History of
Winchmore Hill

A
History of
Winchmore Hill

by

S. Delvin

Regency Press (London & New York) Ltd.
125 High Holborn, London WC1V 6QA

*This book is dedicated to Mrs. Lucy Pettifer, née Maynard,
who was born in the Middlesex village of
Winchmore Hill in November, 1901.*

ISBN 0 7212 0800 2

Printed and bound in Great Britain by
Buckland Press Ltd., Dover, Kent.

Contents

List of Illustrations and Plates

Acknowledgements

I should like to acknowledge the help of Barclays Bank PLC (Archivist G. Miles), The British Library, *The Green Dragon* (Mr. E. Gale), Grovelands Priory Hospital (Mr. A. Lewis), Highlands Hospital, Holy Trinity Church (Rev. Gray), London Buses Ltd., Methodist Church, Metropolitan Police (Chief Inspector M. Priddle and P.C. B. Gamble), MPC Artists, Palmers Green High School, *The Salisbury Arms* (Mr. S. Leaver), St. Monica's Church (Fr. R. Whitney), United Reformed Church (Rev. A. Beeson), Winchmore Hill Meeting of The Society of Friends (Mr. A. Bryan and Mr. T. White), *The Woodman* (Mrs. Underwood).

The following private individuals willingly gave me assistance and, in some cases, permission to publish their old photographs – Mrs. E. Aldridge, Mr. F. Arnold, Mr. R. Broadbridge, Mr. A. Dumayne, Mr. C. Elsdon, Mr. R. Farrant, Mr. H. Finch, Mrs. A. Goodchild, Mr. and Mrs. D. H. Grammer, Mr. A. Grout, Mrs. N. Hicks, Mr. R. James, Mr. E. Lewis, Mr. G. Lewis, Mr. P. Love, Miss E. Mackenzie, Professor A. D. Olver, Mr. R. Shearer, the late Miss E. Spratley, Mr. and Mrs. H. K. Surtees, Mr. J. D. Taylor, Mr. A. E. Westoby, Mr. I. Williams and Mrs. I. Wood.

I should also like to thank the following not only for their help, but also for their permission in allowing me to reproduce from their material as follows. The Library of the Religious Society of Friends, Euston Rd. – from minutes of old monthly meetings; North London and Herts Newspapers Ltd. – from 'The Palmers Green and Southgate Gazette'; The Southgate Civic Trust – from 'Memories of a Lost Village' (reprinted 1982) and 1865 O.S. Map (reprinted 1987); St. Paul's School (Mr. P. West) – Edwardian schoolchildren photograph; St. Paul's Church (Rev. D. Nash and Mr. E. Spalding) – from 'Looking Outward'; Victoria History of The Counties of England – map of area c.1600.

Mr. Dalling and his staff at the LB Enfield Libraries Local History Unit in Palmers Green have been particularly helpful. They have guided me round their extensive collection of papers and allowed me to reproduce Plates 10 and 15. In addition, Mr. Dalling has been good enough to write the Foreword, offer comment on the balance of the content and check for any glaring errors (though any remaining inaccuracies are my responsibility).

If I have missed anyone out from the above it is through oversight and not intent.

My thanks to Adrienne Barrell for doing such a good job of typing from my scrawl. Also to my wife Yasmin for her help and patience whilst I wrote this.

Last, but by no means least, I should like to thank Mrs. Lucy Pettifer, née Maynard, for her help and encouragement. Lucy was born in the old village in 1901 and has spoken to me on numerous occasions of local life early in the century. It is my pleasure to dedicate this book to her.

Foreword

I first came to know Stuart Delvin approximately three years ago. What began as a general curiosity concerning the area in which he was living (he was then living in Fernleigh Road), rapidly took a more definite form and this book is the resulting end product. I recall watching Stuart at work. He was quiet and unobtrusive, but possessed of a phenomenal energy and stamina. Any source material relating to Winchmore Hill was eagerly devoured and absorbed.

The histories of Edmonton and Southgate (Fisk, Robinson, Mason, etc.) all contain extensive references to Winchmore Hill. There are also works of reminiscence by such authors as Horace Regnart and Henrietta Cresswell. This book is the first history of Winchmore Hill as such, tracing the story of the district from earliest times through to the present day.

I have watched the book develop and grow over a three year gestation period. What started life as a collection of apparently disjointed notes gradually began to fall into shape, finally arriving on my desk as a neat typescript.

I hope that readers will derive as much enjoyment from this book as I have.

Graham Dalling,
Local History Officer,
London Borough of Enfield Libraries.
1988.

Introduction

Winchmore Hill is a pleasant suburb of north London. It is built on Tertiary Clay which is covered in parts by superficial deposits of both glacial and fluvial origins. The boundaries of the suburb are hard to define since it now passes without break into surrounding areas such as Palmers Green. For the purposes of this book I have chosen to define Winchmore Hill as shown at Figure 1.

Although now an urban area, Winchmore Hill was, at the turn of this century, a Middlesex village. It had a distinct identity of its own with a history going back hundreds of years.

The earliest recorded mention of Winchmore Hill is in a deed dated A.D. 1319 in which it is spelt Wynsemerhull. 'The Concise Oxford Dictionary of English Place Names' indicates that 'maerhyll' in Old English meant 'boundary hill'. It speculates that the first part of the village's name might be derived from the person's name Wynsige so that the overall title could mean 'Wynsige's boundary hill'.

'The Place Names of Middlesex' by J. E. B. Gover *et al* indicates that by 1395 the name had altered to Wynsmershull. That source also indicates that in 1565 the village was known as Wynsmorehyll, becoming Winchmore Hill by the time it is mentioned in State Papers in 1586.

There have been other books on Winchmore Hill before but none so far has attempted a broadly chronological history going back to the Domesday Book - and earlier. I have tried to rectify that state of affairs with this volume and hope, also, to publish another book recording the recollections of older people who remember the area as it was in the first half of the century.

I have, as far as possible, told the story of events in the words of people who lived at the time, whether this be through newspaper articles, recollections, old minutes, etc., I have also tried to mention many of the buildings that still exist in the area so that the reader may have a more interesting perspective as he travels the modern roads. Indeed, some of the 'modern roads' date back, previously as lanes, for centuries.

There is a comprehensive Bibliography at the back of the book but I should like here to explain some abbreviations I use in the text.

In 1819 William Robinson's 'The History and Antiquities of Edmonton in the County of Middlesex' was published. I have referred to this throughout merely as 'Robinson'.

'The Southgate Messenger and General Advertiser' started in September 1856 and ran for twelve monthly issues before changing its title, in September 1857, to 'The North Middlesex and Southgate Messenger'. It continued thus until December 1862 (after which it merged with the 'Tottenham and Edmonton Weekly Herald'). I have referred to issues of this paper as 'The Messenger'.

'The Recorder for Palmers Green, Winchmore Hill and Southgate' was a paper published once or twice a month from November 1907 to mid 1916. I have abbreviated this to 'The Recorder'.

The weekly newspaper which ran for many years as 'The Palmers Green and Southgate Gazette' I refer to simply as 'The Gazette'.

The Institute of Historical Research publish a series of books entitled 'The Victoria History of the Counties of England'. I have consulted 'A History of Middlesex' Volumes I (1969) and V (1976) and abbreviated references to this work to 'V.C.H.' (short for Victoria County History).

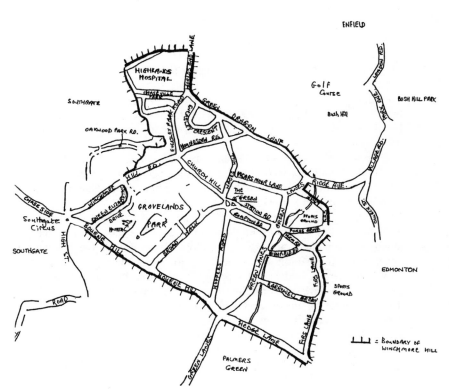

Figure 1. Winchmore Hill as defined for the purposes of this book.

CHAPTER ONE

Before Domesday

The first specific record of Winchmore Hill dates from A.D. 1319. It is therefore only possible to speculate as to the exact history of the locality prior to then. There are, however, some records which aid in this speculation.

It appears that prior to occupation by the Romans, Hertfordshire, Essex and Middlesex were invaded and then occupied by the Belgian Catuvellauni tribe. It is believed that this tribe built the ancient hill fort on which Bush Hill Park Golf Club HQ now stands.

The third Roman invasion of Britain in A.D. 43 led to the annexation of this part of England for over 300 years. Despite the length of time there are few archaeological remains of the Roman occupation in Middlesex compared to neighbouring counties. However, there is evidence to support the view that Romans settled in the Bush Hill Park area for almost as long as they were in England. Their presence in the district was possibly associated with Ermine Street. This road ran from London, in the south, to Lincoln, in the north, such that it intersected the modern Southbury Road (in Enfield) approximately where Southbury Avenue now does. Few conclusions can be drawn about the nature of the settlement and whether it extended to Winchmore Hill.

It would seem that the fourth century was a troubled one as the Romans sought to fight off bands of marauding barbarians in south-east England. The Romans finally left in the early part of the fifth century and the succeeding period until Domesday is poorly documented. It is quite clear, though, that the dominant local influence was Anglo-Saxon. Southern England and the West Midlands remained under Saxon authority even when the invading Danes negotiated control of adjacent areas with Alfred of Wessex c. A.D. 886. The 'Danelaw Boundary' agreed with Alfred locally followed the River Lea. Nearby Enfield has a name of Anglo-Saxon derivation.

The Anglo-Saxons had invaded England as Pagans, but they were converted to Christianity. They were essentially a rural people who thrived in villages and hamlets rather than large towns. The Middlesex recorded in the Domesday survey was shaped, in large part, by these rural people.

CHAPTER TWO

The Domesday Book of 1086

The Norman Conquest of 1066 brought William to the throne of England. The Anglo-Saxon Chronicle records that in 1085 'at mid winter the king was at Gloucester with his counsellors . . . and held very deep speech with his wise men about the land, how it was held, and with what men'. So came about the Inquisition which is recorded in what we now refer to as the Domesday Book, 'Domesday' meaning the day of judgement.

For the Inquisition the shires were grouped into seven, eight or nine circuits. Other counties in the same circuit as Middlesex were Cambridgeshire, Bedfordshire, Hertfordshire and Buckinghamshire. Each county in Southern England was broken down into smaller administrative units known as hundreds.

The area we are interested in was in Edmonton Hundred, which was also known as the 'half hundred of Mimms' by royal clerks well into the 12th century. It is less than half the average size of Middlesex hundreds as measured in hides. Where, then, was the other 'half hundred'?

The adjoining Manors of Enefelde (Enfield) and Adelmetone (Edmonton) in Edmonton Hundred together covered about 25,000 acres. They were in the hands of a Norman who had fought for William at Hastings. This Norman, named Geoffrey, was from Maneville in Normandy and was therefore known as Geoffrey de Mandeville. He had taken over the two manors en bloc from the Englishman Asgar who had held a high rank under Edward the Confessor. Tottenham, the remaining manor of Edmonton Hundred, was owned in 1086 by the Countess Judith, a niece of King William.

It seems fairly certain that the estates recorded in Domesday resulted from the break up of earlier larger multiple estates. Possibly the Enfield and Edmonton manors were previously part of a larger such estate. Certainly both manors were especially rich in woodland. The area we now call Winchmore Hill was in the Manor of Adelmetone. The full instructions given to the Domesday Inquisitors have not survived. However, there is a 12th century document prefacing a copy of the returns for Ely Abbey which must approximate to the original terms of reference. The Inquisitors were to ask not only of the current situation. They were also to ask of when Anglo-Saxon rule prevailed just prior to the Conquest and the position just after King William first came to power and had re-allocated wealth.

The Domesday return for the Manor of Edmonton read –

'Geoffrey de Mandeville holds Edmonton. It answers for 35 hides. Land for 26 ploughs. In lordship 16 hides; 4 ploughs. The villagers have 22 ploughs. 1 villager with 1 hide; 3 others, 1/2 hide each; 20 villagers with 1 virgate each; 24 others, 1/2 virgate each; 9 smallholders with 3 virgates; 4 smallholders with 5 acres each; 4 smallholders with 4 acres each; 4 cottagers with 4 acres; 10 cottagers; 4 villagers with 1 hide and 1 virgate; 4 slaves.

1 mill, 10s; meadow for 26 ploughs, and 25s over and above; pasture for the livestock; woodland, 2000 pigs; from the payments of the woodland and pasture, 12s.

Total value £40; when acquired £20; before 1066 £40.

Asgar, King Edward's Constable, held this manor. An outlier called (South) Mimms lay and lies in (the lands of) this manor; it is assessed with the manor.'

It is interesting to note that the return for the manor of Enfield includes a park. It is quite likely that this was Old Park which for centuries lay immediately to the north of Green Dragon Lane.

The terms used in the Domesday Inquest are open to interpretation. For the following explanations I have relied heavily (but not entirely) on 'Domesday Book, A Guide' by the expert Welldon Finn.

Hide: Taxation had for a long while been based on this unit. It was originally conceived as the average agricultural holding of a peasant household or family-unit. This was nominally 120 acres, although there are parts of England where a hide in reality, in 1086, turned out to be say 40 acres. However, the VCH concludes on evidence from Staines, that in Middlesex a hide probably did equate closely to 120 acres.

Virgate: One quarter of a hide.

Ploughs: A full *plough team* was eight oxen, which might be owned by one person or made up, presumably, of animals pooled on a co-operative or rented basis. Land sufficient to keep a plough team occupied was called a *ploughland.* Domesday returns often reveal mismatches between plough teams against ploughlands for reasons which are not apparent. However, in Edmonton this puzzle does not arise.

Demesne: Land held by the lord of the manor.

Slaves: Probably spent most of their time working the demesne plough teams. In their spare time they could work for pay (which might be saved to eventually purchase their freedom). A slave might have an acre of his own land and receive an annual allowance of food.

Cottagers: The peasantry of the time appeared to consist of three classes - villeins, bordars (absent in Edmonton) and cottars (or cottagers).

The bordars and cottars seem to have overlapped one another as a class to a certain extent, although generally bordars were of a superior social status. Cottagers rarely owned more than 5 acres of land. Some had no land (other than that on which their cottages stood).

Villagers: The villeins or villagers were the highest form of peasantry though they must have varied considerably in terms of wealth and the duties expected of them.

Mill: Ownership and means of valuing mills varied. It is not certain that the 10s value shown for Edmonton's mill would be included in the £40 for the manor as a whole.

Meadow: It seems 'the meadow for 26 ploughs' indicates the number of plough teams supported by the hay grown on the land in question. The 'and 25s over and above' possibly relates to the sale of hay produced in excess of the needs of the manor.

Woodland: Woodland was often measured in terms of the number of pigs it would support, or which would be offered to the lord of the manor in lieu of a cash rent. Since 2,000 pigs would presumably be far more than de Mandeville could have use for it would seem likely that the former applied in Edmonton, especially as 'from the payments of the woodland and pasture, 12s' suggests payment of a rent.

Total Value: The manor was worth £40 when held by Asgar but only £20 when acquired by de Mandeville. By 1086 the manor had recovered its original pre Conquest value, but how these values were arrived at is still a matter of speculation. Finn suggests that the basis of valuation was probably an estimate of the rent which could be obtained on the basis of current population and equipment. The initial fall in value was possibly due to war damage and the subsequent rise to peace-time repair and recovery, but any number of factors (e.g. quality of harvest) might have been responsible in whole or part.

The peceptive reader will have noticed that the 35 hides grand total for the manor does not correspond to the total of individual holdings. I cannot throw light on this discrepancy.

CHAPTER THREE

1087-1299: Forest and Fields

After the comparative wealth of detail in the Domesday Book there is little on the area for centuries.

The immediate post Domesday situation is covered by Robinson. He asserts that 'In the reign of Henry II (1154) the parish of Edmonton as well as the adjoining parishes, was for the most part a forest, which was then so extensive, that it reached from that part of the city of London, called Houndsditch, to about twelve miles north, and was the joint property of the whole corporation of the city of London. Enfield Chace was part of this forest and also belonged to the citizens of London'.

There has to be some doubt, however, about at least part of that statement because by 1154 what had been known as 'the park of Enfield' or 'Enfield Wood' had been converted to a hunting ground, i.e. chase. (It appears, though, that it was not known as Enfield Chase until the early 14th century.) For hundreds of years the chase was owned by first the de Mandeville and then the de Bohun families. Local inhabitants of Edmonton and Enfield manors long claimed common rights on the chase, where their sheep and cattle were pastured, but the chase would not have been considered to have 'belonged to the citizens of London'.

In a charter of 1166-89 the hamlet of Southgate, sited around what is now the tube station, receives a mention. It clearly takes its name from its location at the south gate of the old hunting ground, later known as Enfield Chase.

Robinson quotes William Fitz Stephen's 'Survey of London 1170-82' as follows, 'On the north are corn-fields, pastures, and delightful meadows, intermixed with pleasant streams, on which stand many a mill, whose clack is so grateful to the ear. Beyond them an immense forest extends itself, beautified with woods and groves, and full of lairs and coverts of beasts and game, stags, bucks, boars and wild bulls'.

Robinson explains that, 'In this forest the citizens were accustomed to enjoy the diversion of hunting, fowling, with merlins and hawks and such other exercises, as were common in those days: but as commerce, and a love of industry increased, these diversions were in a great measure neglected, and the forest gradually laid open, so that at last it became the property of individuals'.

There seems little doubt that the forest remained for centuries over much of the high western portion of Edmonton manor. The stand of trees to the north-east of Grovelands Park shown at Plate 1, is one of the few remnants of this once great forest.

In the early 13th century Holy Trinity Priory at Aldgate in the City of London, which had daughter houses at Tottenham and Walthamstow, became interested in Edmonton manor land. Between 1223 and 1248 they purchased 380 acres of arable, four acres of meadow and five acres of wood in the manor at a cost of £215. Two areas of purchases within the manor, at least, were in what is now Winchmore Hill. These were in Hegfeld and Yarildesfeld, both of which survived for hundreds of years. (For that reason it is possible to identify their location even though at this time there was no written record of the village by name.)

Hegfeld lay approximately in the area now bounded by Vicars Moor Lane, Myddleton Gardens, Green Dragon Lane and Hoodcote Gardens. The Priory made a number of purchases in the field but did not come to own all of it.

Yarildesfeld lay in the angle made by what is now Church Hill and Wades Hill and abutted what later became known as Enfield Chase. At this time those holding land adjoining the chase were obliged to hedge or fence and ditch the boundary with it in order to prevent the deer escaping from the hunting ground. It appears that c.1250 the Priory found this obligation so tedious that it let half an acre bordering the chase to William de Forde at four pence per year, rather than a shilling, on condition that he maintained the border hedge and ditch.

The V.C.H. states that a Highgate Street of c.1255 may well be the earliest form of what is now Eversley Park Road. In this same era Green Dragon Lane may have existed as Park Street. A 13th century house 'by Highgate' was probably in the Winchmore Hill area.

Salmons Brook was then known as Stebbing.

During the 13th century Edmonton manor belonged to the de Says, who had succeeded the de Mandevilles in ownership in 1189. It is possible to obtain a feel for the value of money at the time by noting that in 1271 the de Says received a rent of 8s.9d. from villeins for about 140 acres of land, although the villagers also performed labour on the demesne valued at £7.17s.4d. The total value of the manor was held to be £52.13s.6½d.

The peasants land lay in adjoining strips in open fields and boundary disputes must have contributed to the high level of violence in this age. In 1294, for example, itinerate judges considered a total of 10 cases of murder in Edmonton and Enfield. Penalties meted out in those days were severe. Conviction for theft of items valued at over 12 pence would generally lead to the death penalty.

CHAPTER FOUR

1300-1549: Deprivation and Enclosure

As stated in the Introduction, the first known reference to our hamlet is in 1319 when it was called Wynsemerhull. Other local hamlets also seem to have their first mention about then. South Street, between the Circus and Green in Southgate, is known from 1321 and Clappers Green (sited at the junction of what are now Fox Lane and The Mall) is also first known to be in existence about this time. Possibly these hamlets had been established for some while before the earliest known references to them.

Although Winchmore Hill is known to have existed in this era there is little information specifically on it. Much of this chapter is therefore about Edmonton manor in which it was situated. However, the V.C.H. does speculate about Green Dragon Lane and Eversley Park Road. In 1321 the former was possibly referred to as Park Lane, the latter, in 1330, as Highgate Lane.

The early 14th century was an era of great hardship. There were bad harvests in 1310 and 1315-17. 1319 brought a plague amongst cattle and there were further bad harvests in 1320 and 21. The summers of 1325 and 26 saw a drought in south-east England, causing a shortage of hay. All this privation drove hungry people to theft, although culprits were not necessarily sent to the gallows if they were locals known to members of the jury.

It is interesting to note, however, that taxation between 1324 and 1333 was arranged such that the very poor escaped the net. A person did not suffer tax if he owned goods worth less than 10s. From 1334 this exemption was lifted and for some years the rate of extortion was set at around a fifteenth of all moveable goods (which of course favoured those with a rental income). For 1336 the tax suffered in

Edmonton manor totalled £10.17s.2d.

On the limited evidence provided by Edmonton charters there appears to have been a notable increase in the value of land from the first half of the 13th century to the first half of the 14th century. The average price 1220-50 for 36 transactions involving arable land was 16s. an acre as compared with 33s. an acre 1330-50. For meadow the average price an acre 1220-50 was 23s.6d. (nine transactions) as compared with 60s. per acre for 1330-50 (eight transactions).

The greatest purchasers of land in Edmonton in the 14th century were London merchants, the principle one being William de Causton. He was an Alderman of the City of London 1320-21 and 1332-54. Subsequently his Edmonton property was sold to Adam Fraunceys (Alderman of the City of London 1352-75) who purchased the manor of Edmonton from William de Say in 1361.

The Black Death reached Tottenham by May 1348 and Enfield by 1349, the year in which the V.C.H. records the Vikers family as having a house in Winchmore Hill. The V.C.H. also suggest that by then Vicars Moor Lane probably existed as Hagfield Lane. (It will be recalled that it bordered Hegfeld, which presumably had alternative spellings.)

In the 1360s there were further outbreaks of the plague which would have further reduced the already decimated population. From an analysis of tax returns for 1377 David Pam, in 'The Hungry Years', estimates that the population of Edmonton manor at the time was only between 690 and 900.

Although there was undoubtedly a high degree of wood based industry in the area at the time much land was given over to farming.

The local peasants worked the Edmonton common fields in co-operation with each other since by then the custom was to organise themselves rather than be directed by the lord of the manor. Certain fields would be set aside for spring grown crops, some for those grown in winter, whilst yet others would be designated to lie fallow. Each field would rotate in relation to these functions on a yearly basis. The peasants would have the right to pasture cattle and sheep on the common fields after harvesting and during the fallow year. The animals could also be pastured on common wasteland where wood might be grown for fuel and building timber. The local situation was particularly complex because Enfieldians had rights to common in many Edmonton fields and vice versa.

As we have noted, the outbreaks of the plague in the mid 14th century reduced the population. So it was that lords of the manor found it harder to find labour to work their demesnes. With labour becoming scarce it also became expensive. Thus Edmonton's lord of the manor de Say, and Adam Fraunceys, his successor in 1361, broke up their demesnes and leased them to peasants, as many other lords in a similar position did in this period. The peasants were also faced with high labour costs and so tended to convert the land from arable to animal pasture, especially as good prices for wool and meat could be obtained in London.

Similar pressures applied in the common fields. There was advantage in turning arable strips over to animal pasture. This, however, meant enclosing the land to prevent fellow farmers from using it for their cattle. In this manner disputes arose between the tenants of Edmonton. Because of the historical situation mentioned above, Enfield people were also involved. However, despite continued protests and controversy those with vested interests in enclosing (which extinguished common rights) won the day. Between 1485 and 1530 over 400 acres were enclosed in Edmonton. The process persisted until 1537 when the manor came into the possession of the Crown. There were then few acts of enclosure until the Parliamentary inspired exercise of 1801. Thirteen common arable fields containing 1,068 acres survived until then.

In his paper 'The Hungry Years' D. O. Pam estimates the population for Edmonton manor in 1524 as being around 580. This is a noticeable drop from the 690-900 figure he derived for 1377 and illustrates the lack of labour that helped stimulate enclosure at the time.

The V.C.H. states that the wooded area of Grovelands was first mentioned in the 15th century as Lords Grove when it was considered a demesne of Edmonton manor. It descended with the manor, which was purchased by the Crown in the 1530s, until 1571.

CHAPTER FIVE

1550-1649: Wood, Water and Witchcraft

At Hatfield House, Hertfordshire, is an undated and unsigned map of Edmonton parish which is tentatively estimated as having been drawn in the early 1570s. Four main settlements are shown. These are in Tottenham (with 33 houses), the Church St. - Edmonton Green area (42 houses), Southgate (19 houses) and Winchmore Hill (22 houses). Only 170 buildings which could have been used for domestic purposes are shown for the whole parish. About a seventh of the parish was woodland, the best part of this being west of what is now called Green Lanes.

The woods were owned by a number of wealthy local people including a Mr. Leake who, in 1599, possessed cleared land in the vicinity of the modern day *Salisbury Arms*. The largest owner by far, however, was Sir William Cecil, known from 1571, upon receiving a peerage, as Lord Burghley. In 1580 he owned 409 acres and 33 roods of woodland, including Lords Grove (about 230 acres), which had been granted to him by Queen Elizabeth I in 1571.

In those far off days The Bourne was known (under various spellings) as Whappooles Boorne, and was intersected, approximately where Park Way now meets The Bourne, by a north-easterly flowing stream. This stream traversed Lords Grove which, in the late 16th century was coppiced, as indeed it probably had been for hundreds of years.

Coppicing was the practice of growing trees as a crop. They were cut periodically just above ground level and then left to grow again. In Lord Burghley's woods the cutting cycle was about every 10 years and the area cut each year was about 40 acres.

In Elizabethan times arable land was generally more valuable than woodland, but in our area of interest the reverse held. This was presumably due to the closeness of London with its heavy domestic and industrial demand for wood. The local people exercised long-standing common rights to the wood on Enfield Chase for their fuel. However, the local carpenters and joiners would have needed a considerable supply of wood for constructing and renovating mills, bridges, houses, barns, furniture, etc. In addition the prosperous tanners of Edmonton were a ready local market for the bark.

Upkeep of the woodland was expensive. For one thing boundary ditches and hedges had to be maintained to prevent livestock wandering in and destroying saplings. The cost of labour for constructing a ditch or hedge was about one penny per yard at this time whilst the material for the hedges cost two shillings a cart-load from Enfield Chase.

The coppices must have been an important source of employment for the people in the hamlets of Southgate and Winchmore Hill. It appears, however, that much of this was of a part-time nature for labourers and small farmers. Apart from the makers of hedges and ditches already mentioned there would have been cutters, hewers, bark peelers, colliers (i.e. charcoal burners) and carriers.

The wages of the day seem somewhat low by modern standards. For example, a collier was paid 6d. for every dozen sacks of charcoal produced. At this rate Burghley's collier of 1594 earned £5.1s.0d. for the year.

The peelers, however, did not receive wages from Lord Burghley. They prepared the bark they had stripped in loads which were 50 yards long and 3' 6" high. Lord Burghley's woodward and underwoodward then transported them to the Edmonton tanners. The tanners paid the woodward. He then paid the peelers 16s.4d. for each load and kept any money remaining as profit for Lord Burghley. In a normal year the peelers (eight in number in 1597) would thus earn about £2.16s.0d. each for supplying 24-27 loads. Towards the end of the 16th century, though, the peelers became convinced that Estry the woodward was swindling them. They went on strike for a year and were re-employed at a flat rate of about 13d. per day, which compared well with an agricultural labourer's rate of about 8½d.

In 1538-39 the price for wood of 12 years growth had been 14s. an acre, giving a yield, in simple terms, of 1s.2d. per acre per annum over the period of growth. By 1590 this 1s.2d. had risen to four shillings.

For the year ending 29 September 1591 Lord Burghley paid £8.10s.0d. for carriage of charcoal to London where it was sold for £72. The cost of carriage per mile as a percentage of the price was quite low for the time. This might presumably be attributed, at least in part, to the comparatively good roads into town.

Wood-based industry did not completely dominate life in the area at the time. Poaching of the Queen's deer on nearby Enfield Chase was a perpetual problem for the keepers.

There is a record of one deer poaching expedition to Old Park and the Chase in July 1578. This describes the culprits, who badly assaulted at least one keeper, as later drinking at *Bellingham's ale house* in Winchmore Hill. One of the keepers of the Chase was also, apparently, drinking there at the same time!

Another local occupation of the era appears to have been witchcraft. There is a record that in late September 1590 a hue and cry was raised at Arnos, Southgate, to seize men seen to be engaged in witchcraft at Hewes Close (now Houndsden Road). The party set off for Winchmore Hill with bloodhounds but the culprits getting wind of the raid, scattered ratsbane (to put the hounds off their scent) and fled. They left all manner of evidence including a red cockerel intended, no doubt, as some sort of sacrifice. 'Sathan' was inscribed on a crystalline stone. Only one of the guilty was found. He had a picture of serpents painted on his chest.

The ten years following this incident were hard. The harvests were poor and the winters which succeeded them were icey. People flocked to London from afar, though some never reached there and settled in the villages of Middlesex. Thus, like other nearby hamlets, Winchmore Hill expanded.

By 1600 Green Lanes was established as a major road north through the manor of Edmonton although it had different names in each locality. A glance at Figure 2 will reveal that the stretch that today contains the Police Station and Library was referred to as Highfield Lane.

Figure 2 also indicates the existence of many other lanes in the area, the lines of which are followed by modern roads. For example, Whappols Borne (now The Bourne), Sandpitt Lane (Bourne Hill), Hoppers Lane (Lytton Avenue), another Highfield Lane (Barrowell Green), New Lane (Fords Grove), Hagfield Lane (Vicars Moor Lane) and Highwood Lane (Church Hill) leading to Highwood Gate (of

Enfield Chase), which was situated near to where *Chase Side Tavern* now stands. Winchmorehill Gate to Old Park stood close to where Wades Hill now cuts Houndsden Road. Hedge Lane existed bearing its current name. Other lanes followed the lines of modern day Station Road, Compton Road, Firs Lane, Hoppers Road and Highfield Road but their names of 1600 appear not to have been known with certainty. The V.C.H. records that an Inn, possibly a forerunner of *The Orange Tree*, existed in the lane following the line of Highfield Road in 1611.

The Broadway area of today was called Fords Green and boasted a mansion in the vicinity.

The western portion of Winchmore Hill was dominated by the coppices of Lords Grove.

About this time it was apparent that London's water supply was insufficient for a population of around 300,000. This water was anyway of poor quality. The idea of creating a man-made river to convey a fresh water supply to London seems to have eminated from a man named Russell c.1580. However, the work was eventually given to Hugh Myddleton, a goldsmith and banker from near Denbigh, North Wales and brother of Sir Thomas who was Lord Mayor of London in 1614. Myddleton undertook to take water from Chadwell and Amwell in Hertfordshire to a place near Islington within four years of the spring of 1609.

There was a delay when opponents petitioned the House of Commons complaining that the river would cut their farmland into small pieces of bog. Myddleton also became concerned about the financial viability of the scheme and in 1611 approached James I for help. The King agreed to provide half the cost of the works in return for half the profits. Work was resumed in autumn 1611 and the London terminus reached in April 1613. This terminus, just below Sadlers Wells in Islington, was then known as the Ducking Pond, and more recently as the New River Head. Water was piped to nearby houses from the reservoir here from late 1613. During the construction of the New River, Myddleton stayed at Bush Hill House (now called Halliwick).

The New River originally followed the winding 100 foot contour and dropped a mere 18 feet over its 38.8 mile course, though later alterations reduced the length. The cost was about £18,000.

In 1946 the last of the filter beds at New River Head were taken up and the river now ends at Stoke Newington after flowing 24 miles.

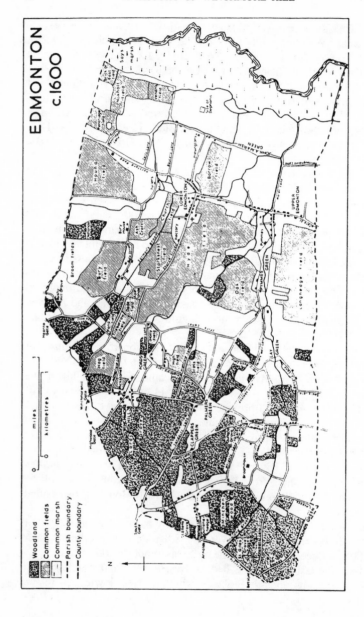

Figure 2. The Parish of Edmonton c.1600.
Reproduced with permission from V.C.H. (or the Victoria History of the County of) Middlesex, Volume V, Page 132.

At the time of writing there is some doubt as to the continued future of the river, which must be the oldest remaining man-made construction in Winchmore Hill.

In 1615 Lord Burghley's grandson, the Earl of Salisbury, sold the 230 acre Lords Grove to John Clapham, one of the six clerks of Chancery. He was succeeded in 1619 by his cousin of the same name.

Witchcraft continued as a local interest in and around the woods, as demonstrated by the trial, in 1621, of the Edmonton woman Elizabeth Sawyer. She was married to Edward Sawyer, a wood-cutter in Lords Grove, despite being listed as a spinster in the Middlesex Session Records. She was hanged after being found guilty of witchcraft.

In 1631 the owner of Lords Grove, the second John Clapham, died and left the property to his widow Mary and son Luke.

Dr. Samuel Radcliffe (1580-1648) was Principal of Brazenose College, Oxford, from December 1641 until 1647 or 48. In the early 1630s he had built a school at Steeple Aston and in 1640 gave two closes at Winchmore Hill (almost certainly dating back to the 16th century) to the Trust for this school. The Bursar of Brazenose was designated to receive rents from the Trust and pay the Steeple Aston schoolmaster. From the content of Dr. Radcliffe's will in 1648 it would appear the total rent amounted to £10 p.a.

Dr. Radcliffe's association with the area is marked by the road off of Station Road bearing his name. In more recent years the Dr. Radcliffe School Estate received rent from the sub-leasing of its land to the Winchmore Hill Bowling Club.

The locals of the period maintained what they probably considered to be a common right to wood in Enfield Chase but Parliament considered that taking of the wood in fact amounted to theft. The House of Lords ordered the local constables to help the Chase woodward John Butcher recover the stolen timber. On 13 November 1643 Butcher set out with two constables, three servants, and a horse and cart to search the premises of the Winchmore Hill villagers. They, needless to say, were not happy with the turn of events and a crowd of 40-50 men armed with bills, axes and staves confronted the search party. The constables ordered, and then pleaded with, the mob to disperse, but to no avail. As they and the woodward moved to start their search they were assaulted. Their horse was injured and its harness cut. The ringleaders included a Robert Pitchley who was sentenced to jail by the House of Lords.

The 1640s was, of course, the time of England's Civil War and Parliamentary troops were stationed in the area. With them came the use of firearms and by the time of Charles I's execution in 1649 the deer poachers on Enfield Chase, some of whom no doubt came from Winchmore Hill, carried guns, powder and bullets.

CHAPTER SIX

1650-1769: The Quakers and Barclays Bank

Edmonton was split into four wards from the middle of the 17th century. These wards were Fore St., South St., Church St. and Bury St., which contained Winchmore Hill. The V.C.H. records that there were 423 houses in the parish of Edmonton in 1664. It also notes that the following year Lords Grove was in the possession of Robert Marsh, a merchant tailor of London. He sold it soon afterwards to Sir Thomas Wolstenholme (who died in 1691), whence it became part of the Minchenden Estate.

It is believed that the cottage adjoining Rowantree House on The Green, and now used by a dentist, dates from the mid 17th century. It was then possibly used as a forge.

The V.C.H. considers that a Chase Side mentioned in 1668 was probably what is now called Winchmore Hill Road. The V.C.H. also records a Highfield House from 1677 and 1703 and suggests that it was situated in what is today named Highfield Road.

This was an era when life was uncomfortable for religious non-conformists in London and the Quakers, trying to escape persecution, established their strong links with the village.

The first record of a Friends' Meeting at Winchmore Hill was about the year 1662 when William Brend, lately returned from America, spoke at 'Thacker's Barn'. He spoke strongly enough to convert Samuel Hodges, George Chalkley and at least one other young man.

From 1681 until his death in 1690 leading Quaker George Fox was a frequent visitor to Winchmore Hill, Southgate and surrounds. After Meetings and visits to other Friends he would go on horseback or by coach to stay at Fords Grove (where Capitol House now stands). This was the home of another leading Quaker, hosier Edward Man, and his wife Elizabeth. The visits sometimes lasted several weeks and involved important discussions on Friends' business.

The group of Friends in the area at the time was probably only small in number. Amongst them were John Oakeley and his wife Elizabeth. In 1682 he had goods worth £12 taken in lieu of a fine levied for attending a Meeting at Winchmore Hill to 'wait upon the Lord'. For being at the same Meeting James Lowry of Edmonton had two doors broken open and possessions worth £14.10s. removed. Shopkeeper Richard Chare of Winchmore Hill got away with attending the Meeting relatively lightly. He had goods worth £10 confiscated by the Bowes Park constable.

In that same year the Oakeleys gave the local Friends a house, tenement and barn on the current Meeting House site, although they were not used immediately.

Winchmore Hill Quakers attended Enfield Monthly Meetings. The local group, in other words, was centred on Enfield, but they held their gatherings at various local Meeting Houses, including that at Winchmore Hill. The Enfield Monthly Meeting reported to the Middlesex Quarterly Meeting. The following letter (spelling as per the original) between the two is of interest,

'To the Quarterly Meeting of Friends for ye County of Middlesex from the Monthly Meeting at Endfeild the 29.iv.1687 –

Deare freinds, In the truth which is precious wee very dearly salute you Giveing you to understand that we have a desire to have a weekly meeting in the town of Endfeild. And do desire your consent and concurrence therein. Also we have intention to remove the meeting at Winchmore Hill from the house it is now at to the house that was once John Oakeys, and doe desire your consent and approbation thereof and to signifie the same unto us by the Bearer hereof and with our Dear love to you in the Lord we bid you farewell. Yor Friends & Brethren in the Truth, Thos. Hart, Wm. Shewen, Geo. Watts, Saml. Goodaker, Christopher Thompson, Joshua Wright, Richard Saunders, Thos. Watson, John French, Wm. Wild and John Woodsend.'

John and Elizabeth Oakeley had by then both passed on.

It appears that about the time of this letter gifts were being made by Meetings as far away as Southwark towards a new Meeting House at Winchmore Hill. Thus it is possible that the Meeting House first used on the current site was a new building or a modification of the one given by the Oakeleys.

The Meeting House itself was used first in 1688 though the adjoining local burial ground, still in existence, originated in 1684. It is recorded that Edward Man of Fords Grove funded the planting of small trees about the building but there is nothing to indicate what the then new building looked like from contemporaneous records. However, as in 1757 there is record of a charge for 'straw and thatch 19s.4d.' it seems reasonable to conclude that the building had a rustic appearance.

Monthly Meeting (hereafter abbreviated to M.M.) records indicate that Elizabeth Man was buried in the grounds upon her death in 1692.

In 1691 it seems that the Meeting House boasted an outhouse dwelling where the widow French and her family were allowed to live rent free. Her children had a legacy of £6 left to them by one of their grandmothers and the Friends had charge of it on their behalf. They asked two of their members, John Freame and Thomas Gould, to take it and pay them 6% p.a. for the use of the funds.

Barclay and Co. Ltd. was formed on 1 July 1896 from an amalgamation of about 20 private banks so it would be wrong to pretend that the history of this giant institution is other than complex. However, it is fair to say that John Freame and Thomas Gould were early leading lights.

In 1697 John Freame married Priscilla Gould, daughter of Thomas Gould. The following year the two men were known to be partners in a goldsmiths firm at the 'Three Anchors', Lombard Street in the City. In 1728 John Freame bought the freehold premises in Lombard Street known as 'The Black Spread Eagle'. I am sure the reader will suffer little difficulty in connecting this name with the current Bank logo.

In order to follow through the Barclays Bank link more fully it is timely now to consider briefly three family strands.

First we should note that John Freame and his wife Priscilla produced a son named Joseph and a daughter named Sarah.

Secondly I would record that John Vickris of 16th century Worcestershire started a sizeable dynasty which included a James Taylor. James's wife Elizabeth presented him with a daughter named Ann.

Thirdly let us note that the English Barclay family are descended from Robert Barclay of Ury, Scotland who in 1676 published a book entitled 'The Apology for the True Christian Divinity, as the same is held forth and preached by the people called in scorn Quakers'. He thus won the nickname of 'The Apologist'. He had three sons Robert,

John and David (who we shall designate Senior to avoid confusion with his own son David, Junior).

Rather than baffle the reader with a long written section on the relationship between these three families I have tried to summarize the links at Figure 3.

John Freame was succeeded in the family business by his son Joseph who, in 1736, took James Barclay as partner in place of Thomas Gould. James's stepbrothers David (Junior) and John also entered the family Bank.

The local Quaker burial ground contains three Barclay tombstones near the wall that fronts onto Church Hill. These are shown at Plate 2. One of these is for 'David Barclay of Cheapside. Son of Apologist. Born 1682. Died 1769.' A second tombstone reads 'David Barclay. Son of D. Barclay. Born 1729. Died 1809.' The third stone reads 'John Barclay (son of D. Barclay). Born 1728. Died 1787.'

The burial ground also includes a tombstone which bears the inscription 'Ann Barclay (wife of R. Barclay, Clapham). Born 1763. Died 1801.' Through the courtesy of the Winchmore Hill Friends I have had access to an old plan of the burial grounds which marks the sites of numerous graves which no longer bear stones. Various Barclays appear on the burial plan, mainly in the vicinity of the three graves mentioned in the previous paragraph as still bearing stones. The graves of Thomas and Patience Weston are also indicated as being in this cluster.

Let us return now, though, to other Quaker records of the early 18th century. Minutes of M.M. held at the Winchmore Hill Friends Meeting House survive and give us a glimpse at local life in the era. The following are extracts from the Minutes for M.M. held on the dates given –

24.3.1710:– 'The Ground that Jn. Broadgate had at Winchmore hill is let to Jn. Freame at 40 shillings per year to begin 25th lmo. last.'

29.5.1710: 'This Meeting appoints the persons following or any 3 of them to draw up a paper to be presented to the next Quarterly Meeting setting forth the necessity of building a new meeting house at Enfield and desiring their Assistance therein and John Brand to sign it by order and on the behalf of this meeting viz. Wm. Crouch, John Freame, Tho. Gould, Saml. Waldenfield and John Bennet.'

27.7.1710: 'The ffriends appointed to visit Jn. Larkins Family, make Report that they found things pretty hard with them and therefore gave

FIGURE 3.
THE LINK BETWEEN THE BARCLAYS, TAYLORS, FREAMES AND GOULDS

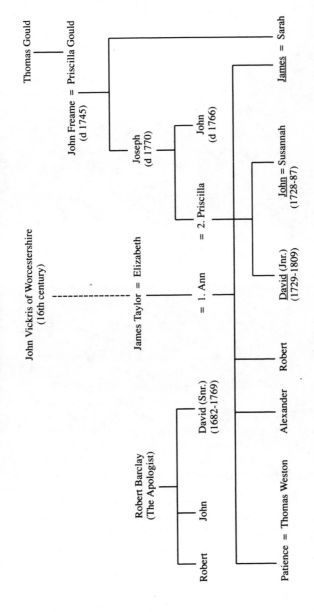

Notes   1. This Figure does not include all members of the families under discussion.
         2. Those whose names are underlined entered the bank.

Plate 1. Looking approximately north-east in Grovelands Park. The stand of trees in this photograph is one of the few remnants of the once extensive Forest of Middlesex that was probably over a thousand years old when the Domesday Book was published in 1086.

Plate 2. Barclay tombstones in The Friends Meeting House Burial Ground, Church These three tombstones commemorate, 'David Barclay of Cheapside, Son of Apol. Born 1682. Died 1769.'; 'John Barclay (Son of D. Barclay). Born 1728. Died 1. and 'David Barclay, Son of D. Barclay. Born 1729. Died 1809.' This family gav name to the giant Bank of today.

him 20 shillings towards the buying in some firing & c. the further care is continued to the same Friends.'

28.1.1711: 'Received of the Quarterly Collection of Wm. Baker 10s.0d.; Jn. Woodland 2s.6d.; Jn. Freame 5s.0d.; Tho. Gould 5s.0d.; John Bennet 2s.6d.; Jn. Warner 3s.0d.; Jn. Dinsdale a year 10s.0d.; Tho. Elkington 3 qtr. 7s.6d.; Saml. Waldenfield 10s.0d.; Jn. Broadgate 2s.6d.; James Lowry 2s.0d. In all £3.0s.0d.'

25.5.1711: 'Margaret Langdale having a concern to visit Friends in several counties desires a certificate from this meeting of her life and conversation and the unity friends have with her Testimony, John Freame and John Woodland are desired to make enquiry concerning her and prepare a certificate against next meeting in order to be signed.'

Turning from the Quakers we note that Robinson says 'In former times when the inhabitants of Edmonton, Southgate, Winchmore Hill, Enfield and the adjacent towns and villages were accustomed to attend Northall and Waltham Abbey statute fairs, to hire their servants (some inconveniences as well as abuses having arisen) the high constable of the hundred was applied to, and requested to proclaim a fair for Edmonton, which he accordingly did in the three nearest market towns.'

From the paragraph that succeeds the above in Robinson's book it is possible to conclude that the fair, started c.1680 by the *George and Vulture*, Edmonton, was held by *The King's Head*, Winchmore Hill c.1700. Presumably it was held on The Green itself. The stay was temporary, though, and it next moved to '*The Cock*, at Bowes Farm'.

According to Peter Hodge's notes on the rear of the 1987 Southgate Civic Trust reprint of the 1865 O.S. Map of the village, Glenwood House, Wades Hill (shown at Plate 3) dates from the early 18th century. (The V.C.H., however, puts its origins in the early 19th century.)

We have further allusions to the 'common' folk of Winchmore Hill at this time in David Pam's 'The Story of Enfield Chase'.

In August 1716 Major General John Pepper purchased the Offices of Enfield Chase and tried to clamp down on the stealing of wood and deer from the park. He was a Justice of the Peace and ordered widespread searches of local premises to try and uncover stolen property.

On 13 January 1717 Keeper Matthew Colgan found wood loppings

Plate 3. Glenwood House in Wades Hill. Notes on the reverse of the 1987 Southgate Civic Trust reprint of the 1865 O.S. map of the village indicate an origin in the early 18th century. (The V.C.H. dates it as early 19th century.)

Plate 4. The Woodman in Bourne Hill. This Inn occupies premises which possibly date from 1727. The house was converted from domestic use when Henry Wale obtained The Woodman's licence in 1868.

at the premises of Charles Henn of Winchmore Hill. Not long afterwards a fellow by the name of William Waller was caught on the Chase with a bundle of loppings on his back and when the Keeper searched his house in Winchmore Hill he discovered three loads of beech and oak.

On 21 May 1720 notices were served on 32 people in the villages surrounding the Chase summoning them to appear before the Duchy of Lancaster court charged with stealing wood.

The following year George Ebbs of Winchmore Hill and two other people from local villages were sent to Newgate gaol for a year for stealing deer from the Chase. They had then to serve one hour in the pillory of Enfield's Market Square. By the time of their journey from Newgate to Enfield the locals were in an agitated frame of mind and horse mounted grenadiers were assigned to accompany the prisoners. They had to remain as an armed guard to the prisoners when the latter were in the pillory and on their return to Newgate, after the hour was expired, to face further charges of theft from the Chase.

Pepper intensified his campaign against thieves but, ironically, was investigated for the very same crimes by the Duchy of Lancaster before he died in 1725.

The First Duke of Chandos procured the offices of the Chase for £3,800 but the locals continued to take both wood and deer for many decades hence. They would have argued Common Law rights to the wood.

The Landlady of *The Woodman* has supplied information that suggests her premises date from 1727, although architectural evidence would suggest an origin nearer to c.1820. The building, shown at Plate 4, was originally used as a house until retired police sergeant Henry Wale converted it into the current inn after obtaining a licence in 1868.

In 1746 repairs were made to the wall of the Quaker burial ground, elm trees were cut down and the wood sold for the benefit of the Meeting.

David Barclay, Senior and Junior, Joseph Freame and Jonathan Bell contributed to the drainage installed for the burial ground in 1758.

The earliest deeds to Rowantree House (later split into Rowantree and Woodside) on The Green are dated 1786. However, as these mention six previous owners or tenants it seems likely that the property was originally constructed in the early or mid 18th century.

The V.C.H. states that by 1752 *The Orange Tree*, *Green Dragon* and

King's Head were all established, though not in their present form of course. However, as we shall see in the next Chapter, it was between 1770 and 1839 that many surviving buildings were erected.

CHAPTER SEVEN

1770-1839: Old Buildings and a Rural Economy

In 1798 'View of the Agriculture of Middlesex' by J. Middleton was published. It contains a copy of Francis Russell's 1776 Map of Enfield Chase that was used when the Chase was divided up soon after. This map shows various lanes at the southern extremity of the Chase which are unnamed but recognizable as earlier forms of Worlds End Lane, Green Dragon Lane, Wades Hill, Church Hill, Winchmore Hill Road and Eversley Park Road.

The tracks which follow the lines of Worlds End Lane and Green Dragon Lane intersect at Park Corner and form part of the boundary between Old Park and the Chase. Winchmore Hill Gate to the Chase is shown at the junction of what are now named Winchmore Hill Road and Church Hill. The Filcap Gate to Old Park is shown at about the junction of Green Dragon Lane (as it is now called) with what is presently Viga Road.

Numerous local buildings constructed between 1770 and 1839 remain today.

Near *The Dog and Duck* in Hoppers Road are some old terraced houses. Numbers 80 and 82 were built about 1770.

Towards the top of the eastern face of Wades Hill, near The Green, is a row of houses (Numbers 17, 19 and 21) which are late 18th or early 19th century in origin. Adjoining them to the north are some old clapperboard cottages which almost certainly date from the first half of the 19th century.

Number 106, Vicars Moor Lane is a distinctive private residence that retains the facade of a chapel. To the east of it is a series of buildings many of which date from the late 18th or early 19th century.

Towards the base of Church Hill, between St. Pauls and the entrance to Grovelands Park, are some old clapperboard buildings, shown at Plate 5, known as 'Woodside Cottages'. One of these was used for many years as the village school and dates from c.1785.

By now the local Quakers were part of the Tottenham rather than Enfield M.M. Persecution of religious dissenters continued, however, as revealed by the following extracts from the 'Tottenham Account of Sufferings 1789' minuted at the M.M. held at Epping on 29.4.1789.

'Taken 17th of 4 mo: 1788 from John Decka of Winchmoor hil by John Scott, Constable, with warrant, for three years. Church Rate (so called) said to be due to Joseph Brown, Warden of the Parish of Enfield – one mare, value £6.6s.0d..Demand 3¼, Chas 8/-, left at his house 541 £4.13s.4d. Taken more than demanded £1.12s.8d.'

The following is an extract of the Minutes of the 11.8.1791 Tottenham M.M.,

'The following Report was brought in and read, from Friends appointed respecting the new Meeting House at Winchmoor hill.

"We your Committee report that the rebuilding the Meeting House at

Plate 5. View up Church Hill with old clapperboard houses known as 'Woodside Cottages' on the right. One of these, built c.1785, was used as the village school for many years until 1859.

Winchmoor hill is compleated; and also a Tenement for a Doorkeeper, and a considerable Addition to the Wall for the Burial Ground, the total Amount of which is £710.2s.6d. which has been paid by the kind subscription of Friends agreeable to Account sent herewith. Tottenham 30th of 6 mo 1791 James Healey, John Decka, Thos. Phillips, Wm. Forsters".'

The ensuing list of subscriptions and expenses for rebuilding the Meeting House included £50 each from Samuel Hoar, Samuel Hoar Jnr., Issac Walton, David Barclay, Abraham Gray and Isaac Smith. Joseph Osgood Freame and John Gray each gave £30 whilst Jn. Vickris Taylor and Hannah Plumstead both donated £25. Ann Fothergill and Thomas Weston donated £21 each, Jonathan Bell £20 and Richard Chester £16.5s.6d. Twenty other contributors (including Robert Barclay and John Decka) gave up to 10 guineas each.

The lion's share (£401.14s.6d.) of the £710.2.6d. cost went to John Bevan for 'his contract for Meeting House'. £191.3s.0d. was paid to Wm. Hobson for 'Wall of Burial Ground' and a further £85.13s.0d. to John Bevan (again) for an 'Extra Tenement'. The work of H. Draper the carpenter cost £14.1s.0d. and there were four further items, each under £10, which brought the total to £710.2s.6d.

The 11.8.1791 Minutes record that 'John Decka, John Chorley and Thomas Phillips are desired to enquire for a suitable family to occupy the dwelling adjoining Winchmoor hill Meeting house and report.' However, it is not until the 4th month of 1793 that these Friends reported success.

The Meeting House is shown at Plate 6. The plaque on the front of it bears the inscription 'Built 1688, Rebuilt 1790.'

The burial ground contains the graves of various members of the Hoare family. (The tombstones spell the name thus though the M.M. Minutes omit the final letter.)

Another building that dates from this era is Grovelands, shown at Plate 7.

Lords Grove, as the main woods of Winchmore Hill were once called, had become part of the Minchenden estate in the second half of the 17th century. The V.C.H. states that Lords Grove followed the descent of that estate until inherited by Anna Elisabeth, daughter and heir of the Duke of Chandos, who died in 1789. In 1796 she became the wife of Richard Nugent-Temple-Grenville, Earl Temple, later Duke of Buckingham and Chandos. Late in the 18th century Temple sold

Plate 6. Friends Meeting House in Church Hill. The plaque says 'Built 1688, Rebuilt 1790'.

Plate 7. Grovelands Priory Hospital. This building was erected as 'Southgate Grove' in 1797-98 to the design of John Nash for the wealthy brandy merchant Walker Gray.

Lords Grove to brandy merchant Walker Gray, nephew of Isaac Walker of Arnos Grove. Gray commissioned John Nash to build a mansion with the surrounding grounds (much of it now Grovelands Park) to be landscaped by Humphry Repton. The mansion was erected in 1797/98 and was initially called 'Southgate Grove'.

It is also interesting to note some of the local buildings of the era which have since been demolished.

'The Firs' stood on the Winchmore Hill side of Firs Lane. The approach to the mansion from Firs Lane was lined with a double row of fir trees. In the late 18th century 'The Firs' was owned and occupied by Sir James Winter Lake who was a great collector of books and paintings. From 1788 to 1795 he employed J. T. Smith, later Keeper of the Prints at the British Museum for 17 years, as art master to his daughters. Smith lived nearby for this period. He later wrote 'A Book For a Rainy Day or Recollections of the Events of the Years 1766-1833' in which he spoke warmly of Sir James and his family. Sir James, who was Governor of the Hudson Bay Company, died in 1807. The house was demolished some time between 1820 and 1830.

Another great house standing at the time was Beaulieu. Built in the 18th century, it stood until 1937 by the junction of Firs Lane and Green Lanes. Its extensive grounds sheltered numerous species of wild birds and c.1800 was in the hands of John Gray, brother of Walker. William Cass bought the property in 1806 for £4,750 and his family retained it until 1832. (Later the Paulins occupied the estate. They then moved to a farm in Wades Hill prior to the building of Broadfields.)

In the late 18th century *The Green Dragon* stood at the junction of Green Lanes and Green Dragon Lane. In those days it appears that highwaymen were hanged near to where they were caught. According to Mason's 'A Southgate Scrap Book' one highwayman was caught near the old Inn and his life was extinguished on a gallows erected by the front entrance. These gallows were not pulled down for months, possibly years. This, apparently, helped persuade the owner to move the pub to its current site in Vicars Moor Lane at the end of the 18th century. The original building there was replaced by the current one in 1892.

In 1810 a modest timber structure was erected off The Green at the entrance to the Wood where two cottages were later built near Udalls. This was the village's first Congregational Church. At the time, and for some years hence, the Congregational Church was known as the

Independent Church.

In 1815 Highfield House was built at what is now the junction of Arundel Gardens and Haslemere Road. There was a fine avenue of trees along the line of what is now Arundel Gardens, leading to a Lodge at the junction of the avenue with Hoppers Road. The grounds of the house encompassed much of the land bordered by what are now Green Lanes, Compton Road, Hoppers Road and Woodberrry Avenue. Little is known of the house or its owners until the 1841 census.

Having looked at some of the old buildings let us return to life during these times.

Mason recounts the story of the anti-Catholic Gordon Riots of July 1780. Lord George Gordon and associates stirred up London Protestants and the trouble spread to rural Middlesex when the rioters threatened to cut London's water supply by destroying the New River aqueduct over Salmon's Brook at Bush Hill. The New River Company appealed to the Government for help and two regiments of infantry were despatched to the area where they stayed until 20 October, long after the London riots were quelled. It seems likely that at least part of the detachment of soldiers stayed in Winchmore Hill, whether in local premises or camped out on the fields.

More of local life in the late 18th century is revealed in the 1795 publication 'The Environs of London' by the Rev. Daniel Lysons. Winchmore Hill was then in the Parish of Edmonton which Lysons described as follows –

'It is computed that it contains (exclusively of the allotment in Enfield Chase) about 3660 acres of land, of which about 1090 are arable in common fields, and about 570 inclosed arable; about 1540 in meadows; and 430 marsh-land. More than three-fourths of the arable land are cropped in rotation with potatoes and other garden vegetables. The soil in general is a good loam, in some part gravel, in others clay and moor-earth.'

There is little acreage left to constitute the woods, of which there is no mention. One therefore has to question the accuracy of the figures.

An insight into the rural life of Winchmore Hill is also provided in the following extracts from J. Middleton's 1798 publication 'View of the Agriculture of Middlesex'–

'The wages most generally paid to ordinary labourers in husbandry in this county, is ten shillings a week during the winter half year, and twelve shillings a week during the summer half year; but on most farms, there is one handy, confidential workman, at twelve shillings a week all the year round. Those who are only employed during hay-time and harvest, are paid fifteen shillings a week . . .

In summer, the hours of labour are from six o' clock in the morning till six o' clock in the evening; and during the winter months, from light till dark: but half an hour of rest is always allowed at breakfast, and an hour at dinner.

A great deal of labour, perhaps a moiety or more, of the whole, is done by the piece. Here follow some of the prices:

Mowing grass for hay, from 3s. to 6s. – average 4s. per acre; mowing, making, stacking and thatching, teams and straw included, per acre 20s.; mowing clover – the first crop, 3s. per acre, the second crop 2s.6d. per acre . . . hooking peas, from 3s. to. 5s. – average 4s . . .

The prices vary according to the bulk of the crop; whether it be standing or lying; and also in proportion to the distance from town. The said prices include the value of the usual allowance of beer . . .

The number of women (mostly from North Wales) who are employed by the farmers and gardeners round London, during every summer season, in weeding and making hay, in gathering green peas and beans, in picking fruits, and carrying strawberries and other tender fruit to market, is astonishing. Their industry is unequalled in Britain, or perhaps in the world. The fruit-women will labour several hours in the garden, and go to and from the London markets twice a day, though at from four to seven miles distance.

Their ordinary hours of labour are from eight till six, for which they are paid one shilling a day in summer; and from eight till dark for ten-pence in the winter.

Their working so much in the open air, gives them a hale, brown complexion, the sure index of good health: just the reverse of which, are the complexions and health of those women in other counties, whose occupation is knitting, or lacemaking . . .

On the whole, it cannot be said that the price of labour is high, for a county in which the metropolis of so great an empire is situated.

One great grievance which the industrious poor labour under, is, the imposition of the lowest shop-keepers, of whom they (the poor) are, from local situation obliged to buy their provision. In the article of vegetables, such dealers treble the market price. Another great evil is, that many of this class of shop-keepers also deal in spirituous liquors, scandal, and bad advice.

The increasing number of public-houses is equally to be deplored. There the poor and thoughtless are irresistibly tempted to squander their money, in bad beer and spirits, to the manifest injury of their constitution; whereas a substantial meal at home, with a little good ale, would ensure that health and vigour so essential to persons who must earn their bread by the sweat of their brows.

I cannot here omit to mention, that the increase of public-houses is, in my opinion, more ruinous to the lowest orders of society than all other evils put together. The depravity of morals, and the frequent distress, of poor families, if traced to their true source, will be found, mostly, to originate in the public-house . . .'

The fashion for enclosing had not passed and in 1800 George III's Parliament passed 'An Act for Dividing and Inclosing the Common, Common Fields, Common Marshes, and Waste Land, within the Parish of Edmonton, in the County of Middlesex; and for other purposes therein mentioned'. This included Chase land allotted to Edmonton under the 1777 Act.

Sales of common land associated with the Act included plots in and around Winchmore Hill as follows:–

To Whom Sold	No. of Lots	Quantity (Acres: Roods: Perches)	Quality	Location	Price (£:s:d)
J. Walker	2	1.2.6	Waste	Dog and Duck Lane)	130.0.0
		1.0.6		In another Lane)	
W. Gray	1	1.0.0	Waste	Dog and Duck Lane	40.0.0
		0.0.11	Waste	Winchmore Hill Lane	
		0.0.34	Waste	Hoppers Lane	
		0.1.37	Waste	Hoppers Lane	
Wm. Eaton		0.2.0	Waste	Private Lane)	
		0.0.25	Waste	Hoppers Lane)	40.0.0
		0.0.8	Waste	Near Hoppers Lane)	
J. Merrington	1	1.0.0	Arable	In Hagfield	100.0.0
Wm. Radley	1	1.0.24		In High Field	125.0.0
John Decker	1	0.0.23	Waste	At Winchmore Hill	12.0.0
John Hobbs	1	0.1.32	Waste	Hoppers Lane	22.0.0
S. Teshmaker	1	0.1.20	Waste	In Lane near Fords Grove	20.0.0

The V.C.H. states that in 1801 there were 901 houses in Edmonton parish, with 52 houses and cottages in Bury St. Ward (the main settlement in the Ward being Winchmore Hill).

Robinson, on the other hand, gives the following figures for Bury

Street Ward and Edmonton –

	Houses			Population		
	Inhabited	Uninhabited	Total	Male	Female	Total
Bury St. Ward 1801	189	14	203	390	494	884
Edmonton Parish 1801	901	47	948	2438	2655	5093
Bury St. Ward 1811	339	13	352	582	724	1306
Edmonton Parish 1811	1157	48	1205	3339	3485	6824

Robinson further quotes that in Edmonton Parish in 1801 there were 20 marriages, 90 baptisms and 134 burials. He states that in Bury St. Ward about this time there were 254 families of which 110 were chiefly employed in agriculture. Sixty-seven families were mainly employed in trade and a further 77 families were otherwise engaged.

The Official Census figures for Edmonton give an 1801 population of 5095, rising to 6824 in 1811.

In 1819 Robinson wrote of the area –

'Winchmore Hill is a large and pleasant village, situated on a considerable eminence. In the lane leading from Bush Hill, near a little thatched cottage, is a well, called "Vicars Well", so called from having been enclosed by a vicar of this parish. It is of antiquity, but what was the vicar's name, and in what year he enclosed it, is not at this day known. The water is very pure, always flowing, and was formerly in great estimation among the inhabitants of the adjacent villages.

This village is long and straggling, and contains about 40 or 50 houses, with a meeting house for the Quakers. Adjoining is a wood of about a mile over, which formerly belonged to Mr. Nicholl, who built Minchenden House, it is divided into twelve falls, one of which is cut down every year. There is a delightful walk through this wood which leads from this spot to Southgate.'

Pigot and Co's 'London Directory' for 1826 contains an entry for 'Southgate and Winchmore Hill – (Middlesex)'. It includes the following:–

'Post Office, Winchmore Hill, receiving house at Wm. Board's, the *Green Dragon*, from whence letters are dispatched at half-past eight morning, and at half-past three afternoon.'

'*Coaches*: From Winchmore Hill, coaches leave the *King's Head* at half-past eight in the morning, to the *Four Swans*, Bishopsgate street, daily.'

Inhabitants of the village are listed. One of these is 'Sl. Compton' who is remembered in the road now bearing his name.

It was in 1826 that Walker Gray donated the land on which St. Paul's Church stands. The Church, shown at Plate 8, was erected on what was then known as Chase Hill in 1826-27 at a cost of £4,249.15s.9d. One thousand pounds of this was raised by subscription, the balance being provided by the Church Building Commissioners. On 2 June 1828 St. Paul's was consecrated as a Chapel-of-Ease to All Saints, Edmonton by the Right Reverend William Howley, D.D., Bishop of London, later to become Archbishop of Canterbury.

In the late 1820's there is record of Winchmore Hill's association with two famous literary figures.

In a letter to Bernard Barton of 11 October 1828 Charles Lamb wrote, 'The sun shining out merrily . . . tempts me to wander up Winchmore Hill or into some of the delightful vicinages of Enfield'. It seems that Charles and his sister Mary would often walk from their Enfield home into the village and were known to have shopped at Udalls on The Green.

In 1829 Tom Hood the poet and humorist moved to Rose Cottage in Vicars Moor Lane. The cottage was destroyed by a V2 flying bomb in the Second World War but there is a plaque commemorating Hood's former presence on the front face of the house that now exists on the site.

In 1834 'The Grove, at Southgate', as Grovelands was listed in the sale catalogue, was put up for auction by Winstanley and Sons following the death of Walker Gray. The front page of the catalogue is reproduced by courtesy of L.B. Enfield Libraries at Plate 10. The sketch plan accompanying the catalogue shows Winchmore Hill Road marked as Chase Side Road and Hoppers Road as Hoppers Lane. The following are extracts from the auction catalogue,

'The principal apartments are fitted with plate-glass windows, metal sashes, and other expensive decorations and comprise, An Elegant Octagon *Morning Room* or Boudoir, about 20 feet by 20, with Sofa Recesses; An *Eating Room*, about 30 feet by 20; An Elegant *Drawing Room*, 32 feet by 20, opening by folding doors into *A Library*, 20 feet square, which, by an ingenious arrangement of moveable Bookcases, is entirely thrown open to *The Conservatory*, extending 75 feet in length; *A Gentleman's Study and Closet; Vestibule; A Magnificent Hall*, about

Plate 8. St. Paul's Church from which Church Hill gets its name. It was completed in 1827 as a Chapel-of-Ease to All Saints, Edmonton.

Plate 9. The northern junction of Wades Hill and Vicars Moor Lane in 1922. Beaumont Lodge was occupied, at the time, by Avondale College for Girls. About 100 years before it had been the home of wealthy merchant John Wade who is remembered in the name of the streets bearing his surname. (Photograph supplied by, and reproduced with permission of, D. Grammer.)

SOUTHGATE.

The Particulars

OF

A VALUABLE and HIGHLY

Important Freehold Estate

EXONERATED FROM TITHES, BY THE PAYMENT OF A CORN RENT,

AND

LAND TAX REDEEMED:

CONSISTING OF

THE NOBLE AND ELEGANT MANSION,

THE GROVE,

AT

SOUTHGATE,

WITH

COACH HOUSES, STABLING FOR EIGHT HORSES,

WALLED GARDEN, GRAPERIES AND PINE PITS,

CONSERVATORY,

PLEASURE GROUNDS, EXTENSIVE LAWNS,

SHADED WALKS,

SHEET OF WATER, FISHING TEMPLE,

LODGE ENTRANCE, AND HANDSOME IRON GATES,

SURROUNDED BY A PARK,

AND SUNDRY ENCLOSURES OF

VERY FERTILE MEADOW, ARABLE, AND WOOD LAND,

COMPRISING, ALTOGETHER, ABOUT

260 ACRES,

WITH FARM BUILDINGS, CONVENIENTLY PLACED;

AND A

COMMODIOUS GENTLEMAN'S RESIDENCE.

Which will be Sold by Auction,

BY

WINSTANLEY AND SONS,

AT THE MART

On Friday, the 4th of July, 1834, at Twelve o'Clock,

IN FOURTEEN LOTS.

To be Viewed by Tickets only, which, with Particulars, may be had of Winstanley and Sons, Paternoster Row. Particulars also at the Cherry Tree, Southgate; the Queen's Head, Winchmore Hill; the Angel, Edmonton; the Greyhound, Enfield; the Green Man, and Red Lion, at Barnet; at the Place of Sale; and of Messrs. Perard and Harvey Jones, Solicitors, 22, Austin Friars.

Plate 10. The front sheet to the Sale Catalogue for 'The Grove' (as Grovelands was then called) when it was put up for auction in 1834 upon the death of Walker Gray. It was not sold then, however, and passed to his relation John Donnithorne Taylor in 1839. (Supplied by, and reproduced with permission of, London Borough of Enfield Libraries.)

30 feet by 24, with splendid stone staircase ascending to the First Chamber Story, on which are three capital *Chambers*, each 20 feet square, and *Three Dressing Rooms* large enough to hold beds, if required; Four other *Bed Chambers; Water Closet,* and back stairs.

On the Upper Story, Six Secondary and *Servant's Chambers,* one of which is now used as a *Billiard Room* and a very large passage room.

The Offices include a *Housekeeper's Room, Butler's Pantry* and *Closet; Servants' Hall; Spacious Kitchen* and *Scullery,* with *Reservoir* over the latter; a large *Wash House* and *Laundry,* or *Drying Ground*; With Engine Pump to supply the premises with water.

The *Cellaring* is co-extensive with the body of the house, all of which is arched, and most ample for the stowing of wine, ale, beer and every article that can possibly be required.

In a large *Carriage Yard* is stabling for eight horses, a double coach house, harness rooms, etc.

The *Kitchen Gardens* comprise about one acre and an half, enclosed with lofty fruit walls, fully planted and stocked; pine and succession pits, and two graperies.

The Pleasure Gardens and Lawn were planned and laid out by the celebrated Repton; ornamented with beautiful flowering, American and other shrubs and plants, of a rare description, and most luxuriant growth. Terrace and shady walks.'

The mansion and grounds were not in fact sold at the auction and they passed to Walker Gray's relative John Donnithorne Taylor in 1839.

John Donnithorne was the son of John Vickris Taylor who was born in Doncaster in the late 1740s. It will be recalled that John Vickris had donated £25 towards the cost of rebuilding the Friends Meeting House in the late 18th century. His first wife was Elizabeth Gray, the second was Sophia Donnithorne. His daughter Sophia married Isaac Walker of Arnos Grove in 1823 and his son John Donnithorne married Elizabeth Henrietta Thompson in 1830. (Their first born son Robert Kirkpatrick was born in 1834.) The reader will note that the inter-marrying of the Walkers and Taylors, and their former business relationship, is commemorated today in the title of the giant Taylor Walker brewery company. The Taylors, though, have long ceased to hold an interest in the concern.

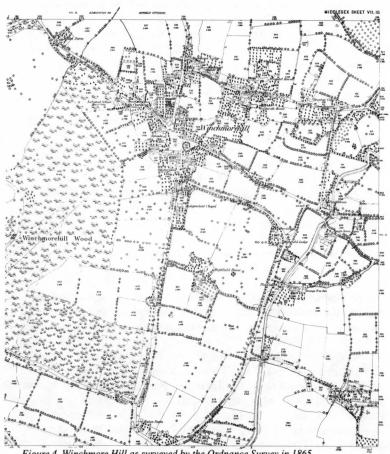

Figure 4. Winchmore Hill as surveyed by the Ordnance Survey in 1865.
The map was reprinted in 1987 by The Southgate Civic Trust who have given permission for this reduced reproduction. (The original O.S. Map was at 25 inches to the mile.)

CHAPTER EIGHT

1840-69: Miss Cresswell's Victorian Village

The reader is referred to the partial reproduction of the 1865 O.S. Map of the village at Figure 4 whilst reading this chapter.

It was about 1840 that the dentist's premises on The Green, thought to have been a mid 17th century forge, were probably converted for use as a shop. It was also about then that the village doctor, John Cresswell, came to Winchmore Hill.

In her charming 'Memories of a Lost Village' Miss Cresswell, the doctor's daughter, states that, 'Before 1842 there was an Independent Chapel where Woodside Cottages now stand, and from the numbers of bones found of persons who had been buried in or near it, it is probable it stood there for a long period. It was succeeded by a Chapel in Hoppers Road, which was pulled down when the railway was made, and was eventually re-erected in Compton Lane, under the name of the Congregational Church'.

The original Chapel was built near what became Udalls by the entrance to the Wood c.1810. The 'Woodside Cottages' Miss Cresswell refers to were not, therefore, those in Church Hill. The Hoppers Road Chapel is shown on the 1865 O.S. Map near to Miss Cresswell's own 'Trois Vase House' which was also demolished to allow the building of the existing skew bridge when the railway came. The church referred to in Compton Lane (now Road) is presently known as the United Reformed Church.

In his 'Memories of Winchmore Hill' Regnart refers to a book on the village in the 1840s and 50s by Harry Cox, who emigrated to Australia in 1859.

Cox was born in 1839 in a cottage opposite Swain's Farm near the junction of what we now call Green Dragon Lane and Wades Hill. In

1842, at the age of three, he moved with the Cox family to the (still standing) 'Jessamine Cottage' (sic) in Vicars Moor Lane, which was then on the route of the Bishopsgate to Southgate coach. Drinking water was obtained from a well in the garden and from Vicars Well next to what is now Pritchett Terrace. People could fetch their own water from Vicars Well for nothing or have it delivered at the cost of 1/- per 50 gallons.

A small distance from the Cox's cottage in Vicars Moor Lane was Beadle's furniture store which Miss Cresswell later described as, 'a large barn of white painted weather boarding some 20 or 30 feet high to the ridge pole of its steep tiled roof. It was crammed from end to end with old and new furniture, carpets, etc. It was burnt down in March 1878 . . .'

Harry Cox's first school, St. Paul's, was the one housed in the clapperboard cottage towards the bottom of Church Hill. His teacher there was a Mrs. Newman. Later he attended The Enfield British School in Chase Side, Enfield which he reached after a countryside walk.

Harry's father was bailiff to John Wade the merchant tailor who died in 1865. Wade is remembered in the local street names Wades Hill and Wades Grove. He resided at Beaumont Lodge, shown at Plate 9 (when it was used by Avondale College for Girls). This probably dates from the late 18th century and stood on the northern junction of what we now call Wades Hill and Vicars Moor Lane. Wade was reputedly the richest man in the village with the largest estate in the vicinity. Cox indicates that Wade was very pompous. His wife was the only lady with a page to follow her to church, open the door to her pew and arrange the cushions and hassock.

In this era the district was divided into fields, each of which was about 10 acres, but only a few of them had 'gentlemen's houses' on them. However, there were about half a dozen such houses without any land attached.

Cox recalled being driven to the 1851 Exhibition at Hyde Park by Newby who had a livery stable on Wades Hill (as it is now called). He also mentioned that living next door to him in 'Iver Cottage' (also still standing) was Police Sergeant Hannon who was stabbed in the neck by another policeman whom he caught milking Risley's cows!

Another local crime occurred in 1844 when thieves broke into St. Paul's Chapel-of-Ease to All Saints, Edmonton and accidently (it is presumed) set it alight, causing much damage to the eastern end.

The 'Post Office Directory 1845' describes Winchmore Hill as 'a large village and chapelry in Bury Street Ward in Edmonton Parish, Union and Hundred, near the New River. It consists of several scattered streets, about 8 miles from London, north, and 1 mile from Southgate, Enfield Chase and Lower Edmonton. It consists principally of villa residences occupied by wealthy mercantile men from the metropolis. The population in 1842, was 2,438. It has a district church, dedicated to St. Paul, in the incumbency of the Rev. E. B. Warren, valued at £100 per annum, and in the presentation of the vicar of Edmonton. Here is the Islington Poor House with 45 inmates. Here is an old Quakers burying ground. Enfield Park is half a mile north-east. Barron's Well Hill, Nine Elms, and Bury Street, are places in the neighbourhood.'

I do not know the whereabouts of Nine Elms, or indeed Barron's Well Hill, although this might be a misspelling of Barrowell Green. The Poor House was at Fords Grove.

The Green Dragon run by John Tatem is again indicated as the local Post Office with letters dispatched at 8.40 a.m. and 3.40 p.m. Deliveries were scheduled at 8 a.m., noon and 6.30 p.m. The Southgate Coach called at *The King's Head* at 8.15 a.m. and 5 p.m. on its journey to London. It stopped there at 12.30 p.m. and 9 p.m. on its way back to Southgate.

The Directory lists Sharon Turner, the historian, who lived at Percy Lodge on the southern corner of what is now called Wades Hill and Vicars Moor Lane (i.e. opposite Wade). Turner died in 1847.

On 25 August 1851 the Parish of Edmonton was divided into four district parishes. Winchmore Hill was one of these and St. Paul's Chapel became St. Paul's Church.

The Quakers were still strong locally. In her book Miss Cresswell states, 'The quaint dress of the Sisters of the Society of Friends was a familiar sight in the Village in the old days, but the only Brothers who wore the garb were Charles and William Brett of Suburban House . . .' (Suburban House was also know as Prospect House.)

Winchmore Hill has, of course, close associations with families of brewers. We have already mentioned the Taylors of Taylor Walker fame. The 1840s saw the consolidation of the Mann, Crossman and Paulin enterprise started earlier in the century. In fact the Company first assumed the title incorporating the three surnames in 1848 when it involved Thomas Mann, James Mann Jnr., Robert Crossman and Thomas Paulin. There was much intermarrying between the families and that same year saw the birth of Thomas James Mann, eldest son of Thomas Mann, and William Thomas Paulin, eldest son of Thomas Paulin. Both followed their fathers in the business and both later lived in the village.

In 1858 Thomas Mann and family came to live at 'Laurel Lodge', Church Hill and in 1867 he purchased Roseneath, set in 11 acres of land by Vicars Moor Lane. In 1865 Thomas Paulin purchased Beaulieu and lived there until 1873.

The first issue of 'The Messenger' in September 1856 retailed at 1d. and bore the following advertisement -

'Post Office. Winchmore Hill. Despatch: 8.35 a.m., 3.35 p.m., 7 p.m. Delivery: 8.30 a.m., 12.0 noon, 7.0 even. Money Order Office, hours of business 9 o'clock in the morning, till 6 in the Evening - W. Evennett, Postmaster.'

The second edition of 'The Messenger' in October 1856 contained the following advertisements under 'Omnibusses' –

'The L.G.O. Co.'s Omnibus leaves *The Crown*, Southgate, for London by way of Winchmore Hill and Edmonton, 1/4 past 8, morn. and 20 min. to 5, evening; returning from the *Flowerpot*, Bishopsgate - street at 11, morning, and 20 min. to 7, evening. The morning journey is continued to Snow-hill leaving at 1/2 past 10 o'clock.'

'The L.G.O. Co.'s Omnibus leaves Winchmore Hill for London, by way of Edmonton, 1/4 before 9 and 1/4 before 6, returning from the *Flowerpot*, 1/4 past 4, 1/4 before 7.'

George Shillibeer had run the first London bus in 1829 having been inspired by French services. On Monday 7 January 1856 the first buses run by the London General Omnibus (L.G.O.) Company appeared on the streets and it is this Company whose services were being advertised in 'The Messenger'.

London Transport's 'The Story of the London Bus' describes the early buses as box-like structures. They were built to carry twelve passengers inside on two narrow 'shelves' which faced each other. There was also a seat for passengers on either side of the outside driver. In addition there was generally room for ten more people sitting back to back on the longitudinal roof 'knifeboard'. The L.G.O. Co's buses were usually drawn by two horses, instead of the three used by Shillibeer's, because of the narrowness of London's streets.

In 'The History of the Parish of Edmonton In the County of Middlesex' Frederick Fisk quotes an unspecified writer of 1840 as stating, 'In the common omnibus the offensive effluvia arising from want of ventilation in hot or wet weather, is not only exceedingly disagreeable, but also tends to induce headache, faintness, and other ailments'. However, in 'Memories of a Lost Village' Miss Cresswell gives a more romantic picture of the 'Little Wonder's' journey from the *Flower Pot* in Bishopsgate Street to Winchmore Hill.

'There was not over much hurry in starting, the yellow paint shone in the misty London sunshine, the brown horse and the old blue roan were at the pole, there was a crack of the whip and a straining at the traces and the omnibus rattled away . . .

. . . Firs Lane and Hedge Lane, as the continuation of Silver Street was called, made an angle where the great rick yards of Huxley Farm stood beside the low house covered with creepers . . . A bend in the streamlet formed a small pond full of forget-me-nots, and the sides of the road on the hill to the New River bridge were rich with lush grass, on which some gipsy boys were pasturing the horse of the basket woman's van . . .

. . . The tired horses dragged the omnibus slowly up the steep bridge, and then settled down to a steady trot . . . On the right, as Hoppers Road was entered, stood a row of cottages with long gardens. Next to them was Eaton Farm with old barns roofed with antique mossy tiles. At the turning by the *Dog and Duck* Southgate passengers alighted, having only a mile to walk by the lane to Bourne Hill, locally known as "'The Bone" . . . Then the leafy vista of Hoppers Road came in view, with the first cottages of the hill in the distance. It was a beautiful road . . . the unspoilt virgin woodland of Enfield Chase . . . The "Little Wonder" stopped at the gates of Highfield Park, where a fine avenue stretched away to the house . . .

. . . The heavy iron gates clunked to, and the horses strained at their collars to start afresh. A row of tall Lombardy poplars were passed, and then the Doctor's house . . . Next door stood a white brick chapel. On the opposite side was the carrier's yard and some cottages, and then the horses breasted the short hill into the village . . .

. . . The 'bus rumbled through the village and halted at the *King's Head*, where the passengers who lived on the Hill alighted, and then took its way a half-mile further to its stables at the *Green Dragon*, in the Green Lanes. It took nearly two hours to reach Winchmore Hill from the City, as it was such an out-of-the-way corner of the world.'

In the fifth issue of 'The Messenger' in January 1857 there is a revision of the route taken by the L.G.O. Co's omnibus from Southgate to the *Flower Pot*. Instead of passing through Winchmore Hill it ran more directly by way of Wood Green.

By now, of course, there was some amount of interest in Science and Technology even in rural England. The following is an extract from the November 1856 'Messenger'–

'*Local News. Church Missionary Society.* A meeting of the Winchmore-hill Association in connexion with the above Society was held in the National School Room, on the 2nd ult. At the hour appointed A. Bosanquet, Esq. of Osidge, took the chair, the room being already well filled. We noticed with pleasure a much larger assemblage of gentlemen than usually attend on such occasions. Members of the Society of Friends and others belonging to different religious bodies were present and appeared to take great interest in the proceedings, which were commenced with prayer. The chairman then delivered a very appropriate address, in the course of which he drew attention to a very striking feature in our times, viz., the numerous wonderful discoveries and inventions – such as the gold-fields, the electric telegraph, railways, and in the manufacture of iron. He had witnessed, that afternoon, experiments proving the reality and value of the astonishing invention by Captain Uchatius, whereby iron slag from India had not only been transmitted into steel in a few hours, but made into a beautiful steel instrument with which iron was cut with perfect ease. The natural inference drawn by the chairman was impressive; namely, that we are living in the latter days of which it has been foretold by Daniel xii 4. "Many shall run to and fro, and knowledge shall be increased" . . .'

Property at this time appears to have been cheap in nominal terms, though in real terms it probably was not. In May 1857 'The Messenger' advertised,

'*Winchmore Hill.* To let, a Cottage containing Five Rooms and Loft. Rent only three shillings per week. Enquire of Mr. Page, Chase Side, near the Tavern.'

The March 1858 'Messenger' carried the advertisement, 'House to be let on the centre of Winchmore Hill, containing two front rooms, small back room, good kitchen, with oven and boiler, dresser, cupboard, & c., three bed-rooms, large garden, safe and convenient out-houses, at 20 guineas per annum. Enquire Mr. Ostliffe'.

The same issue contained the following item, '*Local News. Winchmore Hill Private Coal Club* – Messr. Udall and Child with their family connections to the number of sixteen have during the past year, raised a fund by the payment of one penny per week, whereby they have been enabled to give away 30 sacks of coals to the deserving poor of Winchmore . . .'

The Udall-Child family was quite influential locally. The following extract of a letter from Miss Cresswell published in 'The Recorder' on 13 February 1913 gives more information about it. Where she mentions the 'house recently pulled down' she refers to what was then Mummery's furniture store at Wood Corner near the entrance to the Wood, shown at Plate 11.

'When my father, John Cresswell, came to Winchmore Hill, in 1842, Udall's shop was not in the house recently pulled down but opposite to "Woodside" or "Rowantree House" on the site of the present stables of "The Limes", but before he married in 1853, the business had been removed to the larger premises. All this property belonged to a family named Ostcliffe, and no doubt they were as deeply engaged in the smuggling trade as their neighbours, as it was in secret places at the side of the skylight in Mummery's shop that the hoard of lace and silk was found some time in the late sixties.

When the Udalls moved to the large shop they gave up the grocery, which (as in many a country village) had been carried on in one side of their small premises, and retained only the more important linen drapery. Ostcliffe had the grocery business in the shop at the Wood Corner, afterwards kept by Mr. Adams, and I have often heard that all the cellarage and some passages really communicated with Child's shop, though doors were papered over or hidden. It was all an old rabbit warren of a place. The portico and flagged pathway no doubt belonged to the old house behind, and a shop front was added. Mr. and Mrs. Udall died before I can remember anything. They had two daughters, one of whom was married to Mr. Childs, who, I think, had assisted at the old shop. So Udall and Childs was the name of the husband and wife (or, rather, the wife and husband); the other Miss Udall married Mr. Binsted, the baker. I think she was older than Mrs. Childs.

Mr. Childs died long before his wife, and for a time her only son George was with her in the shop, but after a time he got tired of the old

Plate 11. A view from The Green looking down what is now the start of Broad Walk. The premises of Mummery's Furniture Store, at one time occupied by Udall's, were demolished in May, 1912, to allow Broad Walk to be laid out along the line of the footpath which the couple can be seen entering. The buildings to the left and the Chestnut tree to the right are still there.

Plate 12. A former Lodge in Eversley Park Estate. The main mansion in the Estate was built in 1865 and demolished after being sold in 1921. Presumably this Lodge, at the junction of Eversley Crescent and Wades Hill, also dates from 1865.

village, and went into partnership with a man named Child in making dummies for dressmakers' and milliners' show rooms. The firm was, I heard "Child and Childs", and his mother always called it the "Children's" business. Some time ago it was stated in the "Recorder" that Charles Lamb frequently visited Udall's. This must have been the little old shop long since demolished, as he died in 1834, years before the business was removed to "Mummery's".'

In her book Miss Cresswell says of the Udalls, 'These people were of Welsh extraction, and were the founders of what is now the Baptist Chapel in Vicars Moor Lane. There was at first something special about their teaching, and the sect were called "Udallites", but this name has long since been forgotten'.

In fact the Chapel, which was rebuilt in 1883, is now a private residence. It is a listed building and the front exterior preserves the appearance of a Chapel.

The June 1859 'Messenger' reports, *'New National Schools, Winchmore Hill*. The first stone of the above Schools was laid in the grounds adjoining St. Paul's Church, the site for the same having been presented by J. D. Taylor, Esq., on Friday, the 27th ultimo, by E. T. Busk, Esq.; the ceremony being preceded by Divine Service in the Church, and a Sermon preached by the Hon. and Right Rev. the Lord Bishop of Carlisle . . .'.

Each pupil contributed 1d. per week for his or her schooling. This changed when the Education Act of 1889 came into force on 1 September 1891. Education then became compulsory and free.

The new school must have been particularly welcome at the time it was built because illiteracy was the norm in those days. For example, the earliest Marriage Register of St. Paul's reveals that for the first 48 marriages solemnised there during the period 1838 to 1853, 61 signatories were unable to write.

St. Paul's School up until 1859 had been situated in the clapperboard cottage dating from c.1785 (still standing) further down Church Hill. The building adjoining the Church was used for about 100 years.

Adult education was also of interest in the village. The following appeared in the December 1859 issue of 'The Messenger'.

'The Winchmore Hill Night Schools were re-commenced for the Winter season on the 14th ult., under the auspices of the Rev. J. D. Frost, and W. Wood, Esq.; a staff of gentlemen having volunteered their services as teachers. A room has been taken on the Green, and is open on Monday and Thursday evenings, from seven o'clock until half-past eight. A reading room, well supplied with books, newspapers, and c., has also been established, and is open on the other four evenings at the same hour. It is expected that lectures and c. will be given during the season for the purpose of raising funds'.

The January 1860 'Messenger' explains further,

'*New Reading Room, Winchmore Hill.* Within the last few weeks a Free Reading Room has been opened for the men of our neighbourhoods. The idea was suggested to the mind of the Rev. John Christien, from his visits to the homes of the working men in and about Winchmore Hill. Among this class of persons (too much neglected and despised as ignorant and untractable) he found a latent desire for self-improvement and the accumulation of knowledge . . . among its many characteristics to be commended, not the least is its purely unsectarianism; though the Rev. Gentlemen with whom it originated is minister of the Congregational Church at the Hill . . . '

The rural nature of the area is again demonstrated in the following 'Messenger' extracts:

April 1860: 'Winchmore Hill To Nurserymen, Gardeners and Others. Messrs. Prickett & Sons will sell by auction, at the *King's Head Inn*, Winchmore Hill, on Tuesday, April 17th, 1860, at 1 o'clock, the desirable and beneficial lease, with the valuable erections of the Winchmore Hill Nursery. The property adjoins the *King's Head*, Winchmore Hill, on the Enfield Road, upon which it has a frontage of 232 feet, and includes a newly-erected ·Cottage. An iron framed circular top Shew House, Propogating House, with Hartley's plate glass roof, span roof Growing House. A Small Propogating House. Two ranges of pits, 40 feet long each; the whole heated with hot water pipes, from one furnace, and Munro's Patent Cannon Boiler, with brass patent valves; also Four Cottages'.

June, 1861: 'Winchmore Hill Wood, Oak Timber Trees, and Poles, and Larch Poles. To be sold by auction, by Mr. A. Richards, in the Wood, between Winchmore Hill and Southgate, on Thursday, June 13, at one o'clock, without reserve, 250 oak trees, about 250 long and stout oak poles, and 300 larch ditto. The oak poles are particularly adapted for wheelwrights, and others requiring clean and tough oak. May be viewed the day previous and morning of Sale. Catalogues obtained at the Cottage in the Wood, also at the usual Inns, and of the Auctioneer, Tottenham'.

This, of course, merely continued the theme of a centuries old local wood based economy.

In her book Miss Cresswell described Winchmore Hill Wood as 'a primeval forest of oak and beech, birch and holly; the undergrowth was in many places dense as a jungle, and in high summer the foot tracks were almost hidden in luxuriant bracken. There was a dark plantation of spruce and larch, a veritable fir forest planted long ago, and the children explored every corner of it . . .'.

The roads were also rural in nature from the tone of this letter printed by 'The Messenger' in February 1862,

'Sir, – Will you be kind enough, in the columns of your widely circulated paper, to call the attention of the parish authorities to the disgraceful state of the roads in the neighbourhood of Winchmore Hill, more especially from Mr. Wade's corner, round by Mr. Swain's, onto Sir Samuel Cunard's lodge. I have to travel one or other of these roads morning and night, and I say, without fear of contradiction, that in wet weather their condition is such as to render them almost impassable for pedestrians. I have written to the surveyor; but matters remain in the same state, a disgrace to civilization. I am, sir, yours & c., A. Resident. Winchmore Hill. January 27th 1862.'

Sir Samuel Cunard's lodge is now known as Halliwick House, situated in Bush Hill Road.

Miss Cresswell noted that, 'The "Green Lanes" was a narrow road with broad grass down each side, it was only a gravelled way, and as there were no watercarts, the dust in summer was only equalled by the mud in winter. There was only one roadman in work for the whole district, Old Henny, who lived near the *Dog and Duck*. His forerunner, named Scarborough, was a quaint figure, who wore an old tall hat and a smock frock. Henny worked also as a jobbing gardener, whenever he chose to consider the roads did not require his labour. When new gravel was laid extra men were employed, but it was simply shot from a cart and roughly spread with a spade, so Highway expenses were not large.'

Miss Cresswell further reported,

'In the Sixties, communication with London had been considerably extended. There were then two omnibuses daily, making two journeys each way. The "Red Bus" went from the *King's Head* to the *Flower Pot* in Bishopsgate Street and the Bank, via Upper Edmonton and Stamford Hill; and the "Green Bus" from the *Green Dragon* to London Bridge, by Wood Green and the Green Lanes. This was the larger of the two vehicles and in bad weather had three horses.'

I return now to the subject of water supply. The St. Paul's Parish Magazine of October 1901 contained an article on the old mid 19th century village (possibly written by Miss Cresswell). The following is an extract from it.

'There were a few deep wells into the chalk, and the well at Eversley, sunk by the late Mr. Wigan on his building that house in 1865, was 360 feet deep, and passing through the chalk and gault, obtained a small but fairly regular supply from the Upper Greensand. Most of the cottages had no water supply, except from rainwater butts, and people fetched drinking water either from the village pump near the Pond (alas! I should say near what was the Pond) on the Green, or else from Vicarsmoor Well, which was just above where Pritchet Terrace now stands. This was a "dipping well" of no great depth, but practically never failed. It is said to have been sunk by a former Vicar of Edmonton to provide water for his parishioners upon the moor . . . the water was usually within five or six feet of the surface; also the sinking of the well was a 17th century occurrence . . .

. . . I mentioned just now the village pump. This was itself an innovation of about 1850. Previously the well was open (possibly it may have been a "winch" which gave its name to the place); but a child, while drawing water, fell in and was drowned; and Mrs. Todd who lived at Uplands, had it covered in, and a pump erected at her own expense. Mrs. Todd was a widow, very generous and charitable . . .'.

The St. Paul's Preacher's Book abounds with records of collections for the poor and needy. For example, there is a note in 1864 to the effect that £22.7s.0d. was disbursed to the sick and distressed in the district during the year to Lady Day, 1864.

In 1865 Eversley Park Mansion was built at a cost of about £50,000. A Lodge to the Estate, shown at Plate 12, remains at the junction of Green Dragon Lane, Eversley Crescent and Wades Hill. According to Miss Cresswell there was a mineral well in the vicinity of the associated Estate that was so strongly impregnated with Epsom salts that in the early part of the 19th century Winchmore Hill almost became a fashionable spa.

The 1865 Kelly's Directory entry for the village is at Appendix 1.

In 1868 retired police sergeant Henry Wale was granted a licence and he converted a Bourne Hill cottage (possibly built in 1727) into an Inn. He called it *The Woodman* and it remains today in those same old premises.

Throughout the mid and late 1860s there had been talk of a railway through Winchmore Hill. Miss Cresswell writes that,

'In the summer of 1869, rather to the astonishment of the Village, there arrived a load of barrows, shovels, and tip trucks, and the Winchmore Hill section of the Enfield branch line was begun by the turning of sods in a large field in Vicars Moor Lane . . .'.

CHAPTER NINE

1870-99: The Village's Swan Song

In 1865 the Great Northern Railway Company obtained permission to build a new line to run from Wood Green to Hertford through Palmers Green and Enfield. However, in 1869 financial constraints forced the Company to consider Enfield as the northern terminus. Palmers Green and Winchmore Hill were to be the intervening rural stations.

The Cresswells lived at Trois Vase House in Hoppers Road where the railway was to pass. Miss Henrietta described some of the features associated with the building of the line locally in 'Memories of a Lost Village'. The reader may find the following extracts of interest:–

'The skew bridge under Hoppers Road was a big piece of building. It is where the Doctor's house and garden stood, and for one or two years after it was built the cutting each summer was a forest of rose and carnation poppies at least three feet high; they revelled in a new soil and made gigantic blossoms in every shade of crimson, scarlet, white, purple and grey.'

'There had been much fear in the village of annoyance from the horde of Yorkshire and Lincolnshire railway men brought into the village by Fairbank, the contractor; but on the whole their conduct was very orderly, and they can hardly be sufficiently commended for their behaviour in and near Grove Lodge. A noticeable figure was "Dandy" Ganger, a big north countryman, decorated with many large mother-of-pearl buttons and a big silver watch chain. He instantly checked all bad language in the neighbourhood of the Doctor's garden. Many of the navvies brought their food or their tea cans to be heated on the great kitchen range, and never once made themselves objectionable.'

The intention was to finish the branch line to Enfield by 1870 but the terrain was more troublesome than expected. Five men met their death in laying the track. Miss Cresswell closed her book with,

'It was the night of the 31st of March, 1871, the permanent way was completed, the station was finished and smelt strongly of fresh paint, everything was ready. It was late in the evening, all was very quiet, the familiar sound of the working engine and attendant trucks attracted no attention, but suddenly the village was startled by a loud explosion, a perfect volley of explosions!

Many people ran down to the bridge expecting to find some unlooked for accident had occurred. It was the navvies celebrating their departure with their last train of trucks by a fusilade of fog-signals under the bridge and railway station!

And on All-Fools' Day, 1871, the first passenger train came through Winchmore Hill, and the little village developed into a Suburb of London Town.'

At first only 16 trains a day left Enfield – mainly for Moorgate.

John Donnithorne Taylor of Grovelands owned much of the land in the hamlets of Winchmore Hill and Palmers Green. He appears not to have been keen on the coming of the railway and operated a 'Green Belt' type of policy until his death in 1885. This was continued by his son Robert Kirkpatrick so that Winchmore Hill remained a village until the present century. It is interesting to contrast how it retained its rural character when the railway came with what happened in the nearby village of Edmonton.

After Liverpool St. Station was built in the 1870s the Great Eastern Railway was compelled by an Act of Parliament to run a certain number of cheap workmen's trains to the City and back each day to help compensate the poor for the loss of housing there. In consequence there was a building boom as the 'working classes' moved to Edmonton in great numbers to take advantage of the low fares.

1871 also saw the coming of the telegraph to our village. St. Paul's Preacher's Book records that in this year Winchmore Hill contained 1,780 inhabitants housed in 397 dwellings.

In 1872 Mr. Palmer, licensee of *The King's Head*, built Stone Hall (incorporating stones from the old Blackfriars Bridge) in Church Hill for Mr Alfred Walker, a maker of British wines. There were other notable Walkers in the area at the time, and so, to distinguish him, the locals referred to him as "Ginger-wine Walker". The Lodge to Stone Hall, shown at Plate 13, can still be seen nearly opposite

St. Paul's on Church Hill.

In 1873 there was an attempt at a general system of drainage but apparently for the first five years this did little more than pollute the shallow surface wells which had been so important to the villagers for their water supply.

The subject of the water supply is covered in the Editorial of the 'Tottenham and Edmonton Weekly Herald' dated 22 August 1874 as follows,

'Residents in Southgate and Winchmore Hill will not be much longer without a proper water supply. The agreement between the Edmonton Local Board and the New River Company as to the guarantee of ten per cent on the cost of laying down the necessary mains has been all but completed, and the Company, anticipating the conclusion of negotiations, have already laid on a supply to some few houses from the rising main. In a very few weeks much will have been done towards making the supply general throughout the district we have named; the Company being prepared to complete the work with the least possible delay. The amount of guarantee to be given by the Board will be based upon the actual outlay in laying the mains, and it is expected it will be for about ten thousand pounds. This means that the New River Company will receive in round figures a thousand a year from the district in question . . .'

As noted in the previous Chapter, with the coming of the railway the Independent Chapel on the site of the skew bridge, Hoppers Road, was pulled down. It is possible that a temporary iron structure was then erected on the opposite side of the road. The Congregationalists moved to the current United Reformed site in Compton Road soon after. The present building dates from 1874 but it appears that it is a reconstruction rather than a fresh structure.

We have noted that Thomas Paulin purchased Beaulieu and lived there from 1865 to 1873. Soon after this his son William Thomas procured the 14 acre Broadfields Estate, between Wades Hill and Church Hill, before marrying Thomas Mann's daughter Fanny in 1877. This, incidentally, was the year that Pritchett Terrace (now numbers 19-41 Vicars Moor Lane) was built.

In 1879 Thomas Kelsey of Highfield House offered a plot of land to the Finsbury Park Wesleyan Methodist Circuit on condition that they build a chapel on the site and then hold regular services there. The offer was accepted and on 30 November 1880 the stone laying of the original chapel (costing £1,200) took place off of Green Lanes, nearly opposite Barrowell Green, on the site of the current church. The Chapel opened for worship in 1881.

By 1879 there was public lighting by gas lamps in the village but concern at the poor local amenities continued and in that year a petition with 500 signatures complained of poor drainage, sewerage, water supply and roads in the Southgate area, incorporating Winchmore Hill and Palmers Green (where Sir Ralph Littler of Broomfield was particularly distraught). These malcontents sought a separation from Edmonton Local Board. The reader will remember that Winchmore Hill had long been linked with Edmonton manor and parish. This historical association probably goes some way to explaining the heated local feeling over the proposed separation which culminated in The Edmonton Local Board (Division of District) Act of 1881.

The Rev. Alfred Drought, Vicar of St. Paul's Church, gave evidence to the House of Commons Select Committee on 5th May, 1881. The following extracts from his testimony help illustrate the local debate.

'Q: You became incumbent of Winchmore Hill in 1874?

A: Yes.

Q: Can you tell me what has been the feeling of the people of Winchmore Hill in particular with regard to the management of parish matters during the whole of the time that you have been living there?

A: As far as I know the feeling of the people, it has been one of great dissatisfaction at the management of the Local Board.

Q: In your opinion, in the interest of Winchmore Hill, confining it to your own district, is it desirable that the Bill should pass?

A: Yes; I think so.

Q: You know I suppose practically everybody in Winchmore Hill?

A: Yes.

Q: Can you tell me of your own personal knowledge what is the feeling with regard to this Bill of the majority of the substantial people living there?

A: Decidedly against the present state of affairs and in favour of separation.

Q: Do you know that a meeting was held at Winchmore Hill on the question of separation or no separation on the 8th of March?

A: Yes.

Q: Attended I think by 400 people?

A: By a large number of people.

Q: And I think that a resolution was carried unanimously against separation?

A: Yes, it was, but there were many people from Edmonton and Southgate, they were not all Winchmore Hill people.

Q: Does that at all affect your judgment as to the feeling of Winchmore Hill being entirely in favour of separation?

A: No, it did not affect my judgment, because I know that the people of substance in the place were not in favour of the object of that meeting.

Q: Mr. Buzden . . . Mr. Watkins . . . Mr. Beadle . . . Mr. Busk . . . Mr. Perkins . . . Mr. Pike . . . Mr. Arlow . . . Mr. D. Lloyd . . . Mr. Newman . . . All those are people that you would call substantial persons, are they not?

A: Yes, they are.

Q: If you found that they were all entirely opposed to the separation, would that at all affect your opinion as to the substantial nature of the opposition?

A: As to the opposition, no. I do not think so, because the persons who are opposed to the present state of things, and in favour of separation, are what I consider people more concerned in the neighbourhood. They are of more substance.

Q: Do you mean by that that their views are, in your opinion, more correct?

A: I should say so decidedly.'

The Act received the Royal assent on 18th July, 1881, the first chairman of the new Southgate Local Board of Health being John Walker of Arnos Grove.

It should be mentioned that at this time although Winchmore Hill was still a rural village it was becoming less 'isolated'.

Bush Hill Park Estate was sold for development in 1871 and building commenced five years later. In 1880 the Great Eastern Railway opened Bush Hill Park Station offering 86 trains to and from Liverpool Street per day. In the same year the Great Northern opened a station at Bowes Park on the Enfield line to cater for the new housing estates being built locally.

1880 was also an important year for local cricket. In the autumn some of the villagers, including John Moore, Head Gardener to the Busks of Fords Grove, approached Busk for permission to play on his grounds. Mr. Busk agreed and Winchmore Hill Village Cricket Club

Plate 13. Stone Hall Lodge, Church Hill. Built in 1872 it is the only building remaining from Stone Hall Estate.

was founded (the 'Village' element being dropped in 1912). The club still flourishes in its original home at the time of writing.

A photograph, believed to date from 1881, of the footpath through Winchmore Hill Wood is shown at Plate 14.

1882 saw the construction of 'Maud Cottages' now numbered 50-60, Barrowell Green.

In 1883 Woodside House on The Green was sold for £2,000 and the new owner, J. J. Butson, split it into two properties – Rowantree and Woodside – soon afterwards. Butson also erected Compton Terrace about this time.

It will be recalled that it was in 1883 that 'Udall's Chapel' in Vicars Moor Lane was rebuilt. (It retains the exterior appearance given to it at this time.)

In January 1884 the Metropolitan Asylums Boards purchased a site of about 35 acres for the Northern Hospital, opened in September 1887 as a convalescent fever hospital for ailing children of London town. Patients were transferred by a horse ambulance which ran twice

Plate 14. Looking towards Winchmore Hill along the footpath through the Wood (in 1881?). Wood Cottage, the Keeper's home, is on the left. The line of this path is now followed by Broad Walk.

weekly from the fever hospitals in northern London to the country site. The hospital, with over 800 beds, stood in splendid isolation, bounded by a high brick wall and was referred to locally as the 'Pesthouse'! This hospital became known as Highlands in 1948, with the establishment of the National Health Service, and later as Highlands General Hospital.

At Plate 15 is a photograph of the Lower Green taken in 1884. A photograph of St. Paul's Infants School taken about four years after that is at Plate 16.

It was in 1891 that the 'Post Office Buildings' at the junction of Wades Hill and The Green were erected. In the same year the Enfield and Edmonton Isolation Hospital (renamed South Lodge in 1948) was established next door to the Northern Hospital. The first wards were nothing more than huts but permanent brick wards were established from 1899.

Highlands General and South Lodge joined together as the modern 'Highlands Hospital' on 1 April 1968.

Plate 15. Winchmore Hill Green, 1884. This pump had replaced the old well in 1850. The pump, in turn, was replaced by the fountain shown at Plate 19. On the right is Roseville, for a long time the home of village Doctors. The houses on the left are in Middle Lane (Station Rd.). (Photograph supplied by, and reproduced with permission of, London Borough of Enfield Libraries.)

Plate 16. A class from St. Paul's School c.1888. The teacher is probably Miss Mellership. The photograph was supplied by (and reproduced with permission of) Mr. H. K. Surtees. His father lived at 1, Victoria Cottages, Hoppers Rd. and is one of the children.

The St. Paul's Parish Magazine of January 1892 reveals that attendance at Church even in those days was often poor. The May magazine of that year refers with pride to the village's Brass Band. It was in 1892 that the well known village doctor John Cresswell died and *The Green Dragon* rebuilt in its present form.

It is interesting to reflect that the total salaries for teaching staff at St. Paul's School for the twelve months ending 28 February 1893 was £261!

Horace Regnart of Stone Hall lived in Winchmore Hill from 1878 when he was three. Late in life he wrote 'Memories of Winchmore Hill' in which he described the village in the latter part of the 19th century. In the book he says, 'In those days Stonard Rd. had not been made. A vacant piece of land, which was not fenced and which was known as Eaton Park, extended from Hoppers Road to Green Lanes and also went behind the cottages and *The Dog and Duck*. It was often frequented by gypsies who used to hawk their wares round the village. Then came Eaton Villa, an old red brick house'.

On 26 July 1893 there was an auction of various properties by John E. Pinder at The Mart, Tokenhouse Yard, E.C. Lot 4 was described as, 'An eligible plot of Freehold Building Land, situated in the Eaton Park Road, on the Eaton Park Estate, (at a distance of about 240 feet from the Green Lanes Main Road, also within an easy distance of Palmers' Green and Winchmore Hill Stations, GNR).

Having a Frontage of 60 feet in the Eaton Park Road, with a return Depth of about 138 feet 3 inches. The land is fenced in and well situated in an improving locality, and suitable for the erection of small-class Villas. The Drains are already laid in the road. The land being quite ripe for development. Possession will be given on completion of the purchase.'

The 1896 O.S. Map, based on a survey carried out in the previous year, indicates Avondale, Eaton Park, Meadowcroft and Stonard Roads as all marked out even if they only boast the odd house. The few houses shown are in fact all still standing, some with their date of origin commemorated by a plaque. These plaques reveal that number 6, Stonard Road was built in 1879 and number 18 in 1881. Eaton Villa, mentioned by Regnart and shown on the 1896 O.S. Map, is now numbered 4, Bourne Hill.

Regnart describes 'The Broadway' of today as it was in his youth when it was simply a country lane bounded by fields and lined by trees which met overhead.

Fords Grove was known as Mortiboy's Lane after the local dairy farmer (whose son later sold out to Nix). Farm Road was then called Jordan's Lane after the farm on the south side which extended to Firs Lane. Just below the farm buildings was a footpath linking Jordan's Lane to Highfield Row (now Road). Its exit to the latter in the 1890s adjoined a corrugated wooden chapel known as St. Paul's Mission Room.

Like Miss Cresswell, Regnart mentions Hagfields Footpath between Vicars Moor Lane and Green Dragon Lane. In the 19th century a small Inn named *The Retreat* stood at the northern end of the path which had a local reputation for being haunted. The reader will no doubt recall from Chapter 3 that Hegfeld was the name of an ancient field in the vicinity dating from at least the 13th century.

The 1896 O.S. Map, reflecting a survey carried out in 1895, shows various developments from the 1865 edition. Many of these have been outlined above. Other instances follow.

The Pumping Station by Carpenter Gardens had appeared along with a string of houses at the western end of Highfield Road (then Row) some of which are still standing. The Pavilion in Langham Playing Fields is shown on the 1896 O.S. Map.

Moving up to the heart of the village, Wilson St. had been built by 1895. Further down on the north side of Station Road (then called Middle Lane) there was a ribbon of houses. Many of these (numbers 2 to 40) are still standing. The north-south trending branch of Radcliffe Rd. (leading from Station Rd.) had been started with what are now numbers 2, 4, 3 and 5. Houses had also been built along the western face of Green Lanes running north from Station Road. Again many of these are still standing.

Turning the corner of Vicars Moor Lane the shops opposite *The Green Dragon* had been built, as had Prescott Terrace (Nos. 5-17 Vicars Moor Lane), which adjoins Pritchett Terrace.

There were, of course, other changes but the most notable difference between the 1865 and 1896 Maps is the railway line shown on the latter. Winchmore Hill had changed comparatively little physically in three decades despite this new railway.

The Housing of Working Classes Act of 1890 enabled public authorities to build houses. In 1899, under the Act, Southgate U.D.C. bought approximately two roods of land on the south side of Highfield

Plate 17. The Pound at the junction of Bourne Hill with Fox Lane. The plaque with it states 'Borough of Southgate. This Pound is a relic of early days. It was erected for impounding stray cattle and was last used for this purpose in the summer of 1904'.

Road for £250 and constructed houses on it just to the east of *The Orange Tree*. These houses still exist and bear the date of construction on a plaque.

1899 was also the year that 'Arkley Terrace' near *The Dog and Duck* was constructed and *The King's Head* reconstructed in its current form.

I will close the chapter with a list of streets shown for Winchmore Hill in the Kelly's Directory for 1899-1900:–

Arlow Rd. (with one house), Barrowell Green, Chase Side, Chase Ville Park, Clapfield Terrace, Cock Hill, Compton Rd. (with three houses and the Congregational Church), Eversley Rd., Fernleigh Rd. (no houses shown), Firs Lane, Fords Grove, The Green, Green Dragon Lane, Green Lanes, Highfield Row, Hoppers Road, Middle Lane, Radcliffe Road, Vicarsmoor Lane, Wades Hill, Wilson St. and Winchmore Hill Rd.

The reader should note that some of these names are deceptive. In the early years of the present century there were not only numerous additions, as the village turned into a suburb, but also various street name changes. These are summarised at Appendix 2. A change not covered at that Appendix is that Chase Ville Park has now become the northern section of Eversley Park Rd. (Cock Hill formerly being the southern portion of that road).

Plate 18. St. Paul's Infants School c.1905. Mrs. L. Pettifer identifies those captured as (left to right) –
Back Row: ?; ?; Olive Beadle; Percy Boniface; Ethel Weeks; ?; ?; Albert Young; ?; John Marshall; Nellie Hunt.
Next Row Down: Miss Mellership (Teacher); Mrs. Fielder (Headmistress); Albert Pawnes; Charlie Tancock; ?; ?; Bill Maynard;
Billy Bennett; ?; ?; ?; ?; Gertie Lawrence; Gwen Amsden.
Second Row Up: Cherry Fielder (son of Headmistress); ?; ?; Mary Bryant; ?; ?; ?; Lily Box; ?; Lucy Pettifer nee Maynard; ?
Front Row: Winnie Kerry; ?; Cissie Martin; Doris Woodcock; Ada Bester; ?; ?; ?; Enid Pontin; Emma Last; ?
Mrs. Pettifer donated the photograph to St. Paul's School (now in Ringwood Way) and it is reproduced by courtesy of Mr. P. West,
the Headmaster.

CHAPTER TEN

1900-19: From Village to Green Suburb

In this period of rapid development the village gave way to a piece of suburbia with a rural feel.

In 1900 *The Dog and Duck* in Hoppers Road was rebuilt in its present form.

On Monday 9 June 1902, an area of nearly 600 acres of 'Green Belt' was put up for auction with A. Richards of Finsbury Circus further to the death of Major Robert Kirkpatrick Taylor J.P.

The Taylors had extensive holdings of land in and around Winchmore Hill. Most of these were offered in the sale. The auction included 'The Grovelands Building and Residential Estate, of about 314 acres, including the spacious Family Mansion, with charming old-time Pleasure Grounds, Conservatories, ample Stabling, Deer Park, Ornamental Water, and the Winchmore Hill Woods'.

The Old Park Estate of about 130 acres near Palmers Green Station was sold for £45,000. However, the only sale in Winchmore Hill (for £2,100) was about two and a half acres at the southern end of Hoppers Rd., between that road and the railway line. Grovelands Mansion and Estate remained in the hands of R. K. Taylor's son, Captain John Vickris Taylor.

On 20 June 1903 William Paulin, J.P., laid the foundation stone of the new Institute that he funded in memory of his recently deceased wife Fanny. The Institute, which cost about £14,000, stood on the western corner of Kings Avenue and Station Road until the mid 1960s. Then the Postal Sorting Office moved across the road from the opposite (eastern) corner to the new building which replaced the Institute, although the Institute's foundation stone is preserved in St. Paul's Churchyard. The old Sorting Office building, erected in 1904, remains in use with a removals company.

In 1904 The Pound at the junction of Fox Lane with The Bourne (shown at Plate 17) was used for the last time and the area lost another link with its rural past. The last pinders (keepers of the pound) were Mr. and Mrs. Henry Reed, landlords of the nearby *Woodman*. When the pound was in use the stray animals of the district were placed in the enclosure until claimed by their owners. The pinder released the animals upon receipt of the necessary fees, which took account of the cost of the animals' keep during imprisonment.

The Pound remains today, commemorated by a plaque erected by the Borough of Southgate.

In 1905 the poet Stevie Smith moved from Hull, at the age of three, to 1 Avondale Rd. She gave a talk on the B.B.C. Third Programme 5 August 1947 entitled 'Syler's Green: a return journey'. There is little doubt that she was in fact talking of our area in the time of her childhood. She described it as 'more of a country place than a suburb' where 'on the other side of the railway cutting, were those vast mysterious dark and wonderful woods'.

There is a plaque on Ms. Smith's former residence commemorating her stay there.

A photograph of St. Paul's Infants taken c.1905 is at Plate 18. Lucy Pettifer is one of the girls shown. She says that at the time the photograph was taken writing slates were used for schoolwork rather than pen and paper.

Transport links with London were improving at this time. In 1904 an electric tramway along Green Lanes between Finsbury Park and Wood Green was opened. In 1906 the Piccadilly Line between Hammersmith and Finsbury Park opened and in 1907 the tramway was extended from Wood Green to *The Green Dragon*. It was therefore now possible to commute into town from Winchmore Hill by tram then tube.

The improving transport led to an Edwardian housing boom in the southern part of the area around Woodberry Avenue, as a glance at Appendix 2 will reveal.

This change was described in the November 1907 edition of 'The Recorder':

'. . . Soon we shall have difficulty in re-constructing the scenes of the last century, so rapid is the march of the builder. The "Green Lanes", which once was green with grass for the road, with trees to overhang it, has disappeared. The last patches of grass went to make room for the tramways; the trees – or, at least, many of them – had to give way to the tramway standards . . . The change has been swift, but it might have been worse. The builders of Palmers Green and Winchmore Hill have done something better than build "brick boxes with slate lids"; they have given us variety in architecture and a smartness which is peculiar to our district.'

Another article in the same issue complained of the trams,

'In this district all was peace and quietness after ten o'clock. The shops in Winchmore Hill are shut long before then, but for two hours and more afterwards these noisy, clattering cars race up and down, carrying driver and conductor, doing nothing but using up electrical energy, wearing out the wheels and rails, and, worse than all, keeping people awake.'

The January 1908 edition of 'The Recorder' noted that 'The telephone is an actual fact for this district. It was in working order last Monday.'

The next issue noted that 'Miss Mann has left "Rose Cottage", and has gone to reside near Winchester, at least for two years. The "poor" miss her very much and some of them have turned to Miss Paulin for the usual help.'

Once again we see the Paulins mentioned in connection with kindness to local people and this warmth is verified by Lucy Pettifer, née Maynard. This pleasant old lady was born in the village in 1901 and has spent her life in Winchmore Hill. She says of the Paulins,

"They were the dominant family in the village when I was young and I worked in their kitchen and private dairy for some years. They were kind and generous people. Every two days the numerous local poor came to Broadfields and Miss Irene Paulin would fill each of their jugs with up to a quart of milk. She would also give each a can of beef tea. At Christmas Miss Irene would visit her family's tenants with two gardeners wheeling handbarrows in attendance. The barrows contained gifts for each member of the families."

The February 1908 'Recorder' also contained a story of the opening of the Church at the foot of Compton Road –

'Last Tuesday the new Baptist Church at Winchmore Hill was opened with becoming ceremony. Mrs. Edmondson, whose parents once lived on the site now occupied by the Church, and whose husband gave it, declared the building open . . . About £5,000 is wanted to free the building from debt.'

The May 1908 'Recorder' described the developments on the northern edge of our area,

'The success which has attended the development of the Old Park Estate, Winchmore Hill, has been most remarkable. A year ago, three-fourths of the houses which had then been recently erected in Grange Drive – once known as Green Dragon Lane – remained undisposed of. Today, there is, I believe, not more than one in the hands of the builder ... by September it is expected that the new station (Grange Park) will be begun, if not nearly completed. The Old Park Estate will then be a self-contained orchard city, with its own railway station.'

Grange Park Station opened in April 1910.

The August 1908 'Recorder' carried the following advert for the houses, 'Old Park Grange Estate. Semi detached residences. Leasehold prices from £500 (low ground rent). Rentals from £48 p.a.'

The May 1908 'Recorder' reported the opening of Holy Trinity Church in Green Lanes to meet the needs of the rapidly expanding population. It noted that, 'The land on which the Church stands has been generously given by Mr. James Edmondson ... There is no debt upon the building; its cost of £5,000 has been met. ... '.

In mid 1909 the electric tramway was extended from *The Green Dragon* to Enfield along Ridge Avenue and Village Rd., by-passing the former main road over Bush Hill, which was too steep.

The October 1909 'Recorder' laments the slowness in provision of a local Police Station with 'The fact is we are to suffer for our extreme morality, using the word in its broadest sense. A district like Winchmore Hill and Palmers Green, in which no inhabitant has been convicted of crime, either of felony or of larceny, for at least two years, wants no police protection at all against itself; it only needs it against the rascals who come from outside ... '.

There was, it seems from 'Recorder' items, some consternation at the rising crime rate. Burglary was the main concern, but there were also reports of what we now call 'muggings' and of a few unsavoury characters pestering women and children in the Wood. However, the scale of crime in the area at the time is perhaps kept in perspective by the comments in the 8 December 1910 'Recorder' that, 'Southgate and Winchmore Hill must be model districts. No burglaries, accidents, or fires of note have occurred for over a month.'

Unfortunately life was still not idyllic though. The October 1910 'Recorder' noted that, 'This is a doggy neighbourhood. We swarm with the pets; the streets are thick with them, especially on Sunday mornings. The pavements are simply disgusting . . . '.

The front page of the 24 November 1910 edition contained the following lament headed 'Beauties of Bourne Hill'.

'Of all the leafy lanes and pleasant by-ways of north-east Middlesex there is none so beautiful as Bourne Hill.

And I say it with confidence, for I have in my time hunted up the beauty spots for miles round, sketch-book in hand, but in the end I have generally fallen back on Bourne Hill. For 30 years I have known it . . . In the early summer, when the hawthorns are in bloom and the tender green of the foliage overhead is lit up with yellow streaks of sunlight, Bourne Hill is at its best; but from January to June, and from June to January again, the most feeble sense of the beautiful can find beauty in Bourne Hill.

But are we going to "improve" Bourne Hill. We mean to make it 50 feet wide everywhere, with proper paved footpaths of Victoria stone or asphalt, and a beautiful roadway of gas tar to match; and as we don't like those curves and bends we mean to straighten it generally. Those trees are coming down, and even the hawthorns will be out of place in a brand new Bourne Hill . . . for we are a practical people, and, business is business, if it is not exactly the way to heaven . . .'

The 11 May 1911 'Recorder' contained an article on developments round Highfield Road. It stated that, 'A Local Government Board inquiry was held at the Council offices on May 1st into the application of the Southgate Urban District Council for borrowing £3,375 for the purpose of purchasing a site for the erection of working-class dwellings at Highfield Road . . . Since the 12 workmen's dwellings had been erected by the Council in Winchmore Hill there had only been four houses out of 1,115 erected which might be called workmen's houses . . . In April, 1908, a petition was signed by 90 members of the Adult School asking the Council to provide houses, at a rent of about 8s., within easy distance of the Green . . . A scheme had just been started for widening Highfield Road to 45 feet. At present it was only 30 feet wide . . . The houses would be built opposite the proposed new elementary school for which land had been acquired.'

It was in 1911 that Southgate U.D.C. purchased 64 acres of the Grovelands estate to be preserved as parkland for the public. The U.D.C. paid Captain J. V. Taylor £22,500, one quarter coming from the Middlesex County Council. Clearly the Taylor family were selling off adjacent strips of the Woods at the same time, the changes being documented by 'The Recorder'.

The 23 May 1912 'Recorder' notes that, 'The axe has begun its work again; the powers of destruction are let loose upon Winchmore Hill Woods – the pride of the whole district – and noble old trees are falling daily. The contractor . . . is . . . carrying out the work he has undertaken to do . . . we cannot bear . . . the groans of the noble elms as, one after the other, they are uprooted, nor the crash of the falling walls and roofs of the centuries old house at Wood Corner, lately known as Mummery's, without a regret that borders on anger . . . The keeper's cottage near Wood Corner is dismantled, the elms in full foliage lie prostrate, the footpath – the finest in all North Middlesex – is scarified by the wheels of heavy vehicles; we are losing a great asset which we shall never regain . . . Fortunately, a sixth part of this old wood and park has been preserved to the public use forever . . . '.

A view from The Green prior to this work, looking towards Mummery's, is at Plate 11. The footpath next to Mummery's traversed the Wood and its line is now followed by Broad Walk.

The 1 August 1912 issue contained the story that, 'The Recorder is informed, on very high authority, that the 'bus company will commence a service of motor 'buses to Enfield, through Winchmore Hill, shortly, probably today. Arrangements have been made this week for a station . . . The through service of electric tramcars from Euston Road to Enfield commenced running today . . . With the two services going, the fight for traffic is likely to be interesting.'

On 12 April 1913 The Lord Mayor of London, Sir David Burnett, opened Grovelands Park. The Park's initial 64 acres was added to by purchases into the mid 1930s.

It was in the same year that estimates totalling £2,587 were accepted and the Vicarage built in Church Hill on land given by William Paulin. He also gave an adjoining plot for the possible future enlargement of the school playground. A few year earlier he had given Holy Trinity Church its Vicarage.

The 5 June 1913 'Recorder' included the interesting comment, 'This brings me to the question . . . whether we have seen the last of the £50 a year houses in our midst . . . It costs a lot of money nowadays to build a house, and the tendency is all against the ordinary man buying one. Ten or twelve years ago every one was for buying a house to live in . . . During the past ten years the average fall in the selling value of suburban houses is 25 per cent . . . The renters get the best of the bargain for they get lower rents, and lower rents spell falls in capital value. I think that is the reason why the average householder is fighting shy of houseowning . . . For the past two or three years the most successful builders have been those who have built houses to let at from £30 to £40 a year, and this is the type which is now being largely built in our district, because it not only attracts occupiers but purchasers.'

The same issue reported that, 'We are now in the season of tar painting of the roads, when the whole district will be disinfected with tar and the dust terror will be abolished. The following is a complete list of the roads and paths which are to be tar painted very shortly:– Green Lanes, . . . Winchmore Hill Road (about 100 yards), Bourne Hill (about 100 yards), Station Road, The Green, Compton Road and Hoppers Road, Green Dragon Lane (Green Lanes to Old Park Ridings), Wades Hill (from The Green to Vicarsmoor Lane). . .'.

The 28 August 1913 'Recorder' reported the opening of the Public Baths in Barrowell Green whilst the 9 April 1914 issue spoke of the 'handsome new school in Highfield Road, known as the "Winchmore" Council School . . .'.

The 7 May 1914 'Recorder' front page gave pride of place to the opening of St. Monica's Church. 'The church . . . was filled some time before the hour of service, many late arrivals being unable to find a seat. Two suffragettes stationed themselves at the entrance gates distributing leaflets . . .'

Suffragettes are mentioned again on the front page of the 18 June 1914 issue as follows.

'There were lively scenes at Palmers Green Triangle on Saturday night, when a party of local suffragettes was mobbed, and prevented from holding a meeting . . . eggs and flour were thrown, Mr. Goulden (ex-secretary of the Winchmore Hill Ratepayers' Association, and a brother of Mrs. Pankhurst) was knocked down, and one lady was roughly handled . . . Several policemen, both in uniform and in plain clothes, were present, and doubtless seeing that the crowd was bent on mischief, a police sergeant came to Mr. Goulden's rescue, and escorted him in the direction of Fox Lane, followed by a jeering mob.

At the *Fox Tavern* Mr. Goulden boarded a tram car, followed by the policeman, but the crowd was not so easily shaken off, and many climbed on the car, while others followed on bicycles . . .

. . . Mr. Goulden, on arriving at Winchmore Hill, parted company with his police protector, but soon realised that his persecutors had not been left behind. A large crowd soon gathered in the Broadway, and Councillor Willis and Councillor Sadler, both magistrates, appeared on the scene. Councillor Willis persuaded Mr. Goulden . . . to return with him to his house in Station Road. Members of the crowd, however, visited Radcliffe Road and made a demonstration in front of Mr. Goulden's house, hurling eggs through an open window. The arrival of police prevented any further damage.

Before 11 o'clock the crowd melted away, and Mr. and Mrs. Goulden were able to return to their home without further molestation . . .'

An old photograph of The Green, probably taken in 1914 at the latest, is shown at Plate 19.

August 1914 saw the declaration of War and recruiting offices were set up at Edmonton and Southgate Town Halls. Full page adverts appeared in local papers urging men to join their local battalion – The Middlesex Regiment. Many of the local horses were commandeered by the Military for transportation purposes.

The 5 November 1914 'Recorder' noted that, 'The committee in charge of the scheme for housing Belgian refugees at Beaulieu, cannot be said to have wasted time, for within a week the house had been leased, the workman put in, and everything was in full swing for the reception of the new comers.

As the house had been unoccupied for four years, it goes without saying that there was much to be done. It is a fine house with some handsome reception rooms in it, a magnificent old cedar shading the lawn in front, and the New River flowing at the bottom of the back garden . . .'.

186, Hoppers Road, was also used to accommodate Belgian refugees.

The 3 December 1914 'Recorder' contained news of another local mansion adapted for the war effort.

'At Roseneath Voluntary Hospital we have a striking example of good work which seeks no praise and no reward beyond that which always comes to good work well done. The mansion has been fitted up as a military hospital, regardless of expense, by a local benefactor who desires to remain anonymous. The medical staff, the nursing staff – all, in fact, except a few of the kitchen assistants – are sacrificing good

Plate 19. The fountain in the Lower Green. In the background are (on the left) the old Mission Hall on the western junction of The Green and Wilson St. On the opposite corner is 'Grove Lodge' which for some years was the home of Dr. Goble. The picture is undated, but judging from the dress, presumably it was taken before 1914.

incomes and giving their valuable services free. They, too, desire to remain anonymous . . .'

The War flavour also comes across in the following extracts from 'The Gazette' –

18 September 1915. 'On Sunday evening at St. Paul's Church, the Vicar told his parishioners that those who were nervous might find a refuge in the basement of the Institute. He pointed out how remote are the chances of injury by Zeppelins. We can't, however, get away from the fact that there are many nervous people to whom such a refuge would afford a great relief.'

27 November 1915. 'From Wilson St. – which, by the way, has only 18 houses – 12 men have joined the Colours at various times. Of that number five have paid the great sacrifice and two are wounded. One of the most recent deaths reported is that of Fred Clarke, who in civilian life was a clerk in the Clearing House. He was also a well-known member of the Winchmore Hill Cricket Club, a member of St. Paul's Church and more recently assisted as organist at St. Paul's Mission. He enlisted at the beginning of the War, and was soon promoted to corporal, acting as an instructor in a hand grenade school. He leaves a widowed mother, with whom great sympathy is felt on all hands.'

24 June 1916 'Grovelands. Southgate Auxiliary War Hospital. Official Opening. The fine old mansion, Grovelands House, which has been generously placed by Capt. J. V. Taylor at the disposal of the Southgate Branch of the Middlesex Voluntary Aid Organisation, was officially opened on Saturday afternoon. It was the first day of the month on which anything like summer weather prevailed, and the people came in their thousands not only from all parts of the immediate district, but from Enfield, Wood Green, and other adjoining localities . . . '

The following are some recollections by local people of one event in the Great War that appears to have stayed in the mind.

Mrs. Lucy Pettifer says, "I remember the night in September, 1916 when Captain Leefe Robinson shot down the Zeppelin, which landed at Cuffley. The flames lit up the sky for miles around and all the villagers stood and cheered."

The late Miss E. Spratley's father was the resident engineer at the Northern Hospital (later called Highlands). She was born there in 1904 and raised on the premises. In October 1986 she commented, "A vivid memory of my childhood was the night during the Great War that a

Zeppelin was shot down near Cuffley. I recall that the light from the flames would have been sufficient to allow me to read a book without recourse to any other form of illumination. My father was in the equivalent of the Home Guard and had to act as sentry to the stricken airship the following day. He found the stench awful."

However 'ordinary life' continued for some. 'The Gazette' still carried advertisements under the 'Domestic Servants' column. Examples are –

20 March 1915 'General Servant Wanted; wages £16 to £20; age 20-30 Plain cooking: 4 in family; no children. Alternate Sundays and evening weekly – 42, Compton Rd.'

17 July 1915 'Good general servant; Comfortable home; wages £20 to £24 per year – Apply Mrs. Bruton. The Limes, Hedge-Lane, Palmers Green.'

4 December 1915 'Clean, trustworthy girl wanted for housework every morning. – Call any morning 32 Radcliffe Road.'

'Ordinary life' was still also partly rural in nature. The 12 June 1915 'Gazette' contained the advertisement,

'*Stone Hall Herd of Dairy Cows.* Milk from this herd delivered in sealed bottles twice daily within one hour of milking . . . For all particulars apply to Mr. A. Partridge, Woodside Cottage, Church Hill.'

Development was also continuing, as evidenced by the following from 'The Gazette' of 31 July, 1915,

'*Denleigh Gardens.* The (Council) Surveyor reported that the length of road extending from Branscombe Gardens to Seaforth Gardens had been completed, and that a balance of £220 out of £600 which the Council had agreed to contribute was due to Messrs. Byford and Wilson . . .'

There was a considerable gap between the laying out of the roads and their habitation. Branscombe Gardens and Seaforth Gardens first appear listed in the 1922 Kelly's Directory whilst Denleigh Gardens is not indicated as having residents until a number of years after this. Indeed there is something a little curious about the snippet in the 9 December 1915 'Recorder' that ran, 'Mr. Charles Woods, aged 75, of Broad Walk, Winchmore Hill, is now lying in the Wood Green Hospital suffering from a fractured leg . . .'. The first proper listing of Broad Walk in a Kelly's Directory is in the 1922 edition!

Broad Walk receives another mention in the following extract from 'The Recorder' of 13 January 1916.

'A long-felt want has been supplied by the opening of the smart new police station near St. Bartholomew's Hospital Athletic Ground. The opening was a purely informal affair, the men stationed there taking up their new duties at six o'clock on the morning of December 13th (1915) as if nothing unusual had happened.

The new station will be the centre of a newly mapped out police district extending from the golf links on the north to Alderman's Hill on the south, and as far west as Ulleswater Road and part of Broad Walk . . .'

The land on which the Police Station was built had once been part of the large Highfield Park Estate. The Police had purchased the plot from the London Brick Company for £1,215 as long ago as 8 January 1907 and there had been numerous complaints in 'The Recorder' over the years concerning the delay between purchase of the land and opening of the Station.

A feel for the price of property at that time can be gained from the following entry in 'The Gazette' of 25 March, 1916,

'To be sold, freehold, semi-detached house, 2 reception rooms, kitchen, and offices, 4 bedrooms; excellent conditions; electric light; nice garden; road charges paid. Splendid position near station and trams. £735 – Apply Owner, "Clovelly", Orpington Road, Winchmore Hill, N.'

The War, of course, ended in 1918, the year that Palmers Green High School moved with about 300 pupils from Palmers Green to the Avondale Hall premises it currently occupies in Hoppers Road.

We close the Chapter with Winchmore Hill as a green suburb of London. The next two decades were to see much of the greenness go, along with many of the old mansions.

CHAPTER ELEVEN

1920-38: Urbanisation Completed

During this period the urbanisation of Winchmore Hill continued such that by the outbreak of the last World War it was physically much as it is today. This urbanisation process was, of course, not unique to the area at the time. The phenomenon was common throughout what are now the suburbs of Outer London.

The inter-War era was one of great depression throughout much of Great Britain. The old industries of shipbuilding, etc., were in decline in the North but in the South East there was a boom in light mass production industry. Razor blades, radios, vacuum cleaners and such like were all made in the Greater London area. In addition there was an increase in the number of large Corporations, many of whom had headquarters in the Capital. Further, there was an increasing amount of Government legislation and intervention, so requiring more Civil Servants. Local Government was expanding. All this not only gave a demand for unskilled manual labour, but also white collar workers. Between 1923 and 1939 something like two-thirds of the new jobs in Great Britain were created in Greater London. Between the wars London's population rose by about one and a half million, of which over one third were 'migrants' from other parts of Britain.

Not only was there an increased demand for housing for all types of working people, there was also a change in attitudes to ownership. Before the Great War most people rented their accommodation but after the conflict there was growth and development of the now familiar Building Societies. These provided a safe haven for people's savings in what generally seemed to be an unsafe world and this attraction was aided by a tax concession on interest paid. Further, people were marrying earlier in life. There was therefore a great increase in the demand for homes for people to call their own.

Land was relatively cheap on the outskirts of London because agriculture was depressed and so there was rapid development of outer suburbs. Often Building Societies would liaise with local builders in buying up land and erecting new housing estates with finances arranged in such a way that first time buyers had to put down only a 5% deposit. Indeed, with so much development (i.e. supply) using fairly cheap material and low cost labour (for there were always people from depressed areas willing to step into low paid building work) house prices actually fell in the early 1930s (in real terms) to a very low level. The following advertisement in 'The Gazette' of 2 January 1931 demonstrates the point,

'£50 down. Suitable for flats; Winchmore Hill, Elm Park Road; 10-roomed house, with fine garden; electric light; redecorated throughout; 68 years' lease; £10 g.r.; £975 - Apply, King & Co., The Broadway, N.21. 'Phone: Palmers Green 0838.'

In the inter-War period most of the old Winchmore Hill mansions came on the market and their estates were turned over to middle class housing. The first one of these, to start the trend, was Ford's Grove which stood where Capitol House and the Nat West Bank are today on Green Lanes. The following article in 'The Gazette' of 8 May, 1920 is interesting since not only does it give a short history of the house and its occupants, it also talks of Winchmore Hill Cricket Club.

'Many of our readers who are old residents of Winchmore Hill will have read in our last issue, with feelings mixed with regret, of the impending sale by auction of Ford's Grove estate. Some few weeks since we referred to the demolition of the fine old residence of which then only a few heaps of brick rubble remained. Now all is cleared off, and the site leaves no trace of a residence which had been the most important of the most charming woodland village in Middlesex. The advertisement tells us that "the estate comprises ripe building land with frontages to Green Lanes and other public roads; eminent pasture and accommodation land eminently suitable for recreation or sports grounds, or for nurseries."

The property came into the Busk family in the early years of the last century through the marriage of Mr. Edward Busk to Miss Thomasine Teshmaker, younger daughter of Mrs. Teshmaker. Mr. Edward Busk, who was a barrister-at-law, lived in the vicinity of Bedford Row, and after the birth of three children, Mrs. Teshmaker gave up Ford's Grove about 1808 and removed to another house at Winchmore Hill; her son-in-law and daughter succeeding her. Mr. Teshmaker Busk was the last of the Busks who resided at Ford's Grove. He married Miss Mary Ackworth in 1885, and it is said she did not like her new home: anyhow, for some reason or another they left in a few years, and Ford's Grove was tenanted by several people who were more or less strangers to the district.

For many years it had remained unoccupied, and had obviously fallen greatly into dilapidation. Mr. Thomas Teshmaker Busk died a few years after he gave up his residence at Winchmore Hill, leaving a family of several children. The eldest, Edward Teshmaker Busk, became an engineer, and celebrated himself as an inventor of aeroplanes, and finally met with an appallingly tragic death. Another brother was killed while bombing the Turks from an aeroplane in Gallipoli.

The Busks were important residents of Winchmore Hill, and were Justices of the Peace in those days, regularly attending the Edmonton Petty Sessions. They were kind and thoughtful of the welfare of their poorer neighbours, and were held in high esteem by all classes of the community.

The venerable Winchmore Hill cricketer, Mr. John Moore, occupied the position of head gardener when his master gave up occupation of Ford's Grove. It was he who started the Winchmore Hill Cricket Club, Mr. Busk giving free use of the cricket field. The club has played on the same ground ever since, now upwards of 30 years, and has become one of the most important cricket clubs in the district. Of course, the sale of this property will be nothing short of a misfortune to those who have enjoyed the use of it for so many years. Mr. John Moore is near upon 70 years of age, but is still enthusiastic in the game as he was in the far-off years when he obtained the generous concession from his master and founded the club.

The advertisement foreshadows the future of Ford's Grove, which in the course of a few years will exist only as a name.'

Winchmore Hill Cricket Club celebrated its centenary in 1980 and still plays on the grounds to the east of the New River where it started, on what was then part of the Ford's Grove Estate. These grounds were purchased by W. T. Paulin at the auction of the Estate on 10 May 1920 for £8,000. He was knighted in 1929 but died in 1931. The land was leased to the Club by his daughter Irene who survived until 1960.

Under the terms of her Will the Club was granted a 99 year lease at a yearly rent of one shilling (5p) and provision made that the land remain a recreation ground in perpetuity.

On 21 July 1920 415 acres of land to the northern boundary of area was sold off, including Chaseville Park in Winchmore Hill.

It was in 1920 that J. V. Taylor sold Grovelands Mansion and 13.60 acres of surrounding land to the Middlesex V.A.O. for £10,000. At the same time he sold an adjoining area to the north west to the Great Northern Central Hospital for £2,574. The V.A.O. made the mansion available to the Great Northern Central as a hospital of recovery in the same year.

On 29 November 1921 E. J. Westoby, in conjunction with Maple & Co., auctioned Eversley Park Mansion and its 36 acre Estate of well-timbered parklands. The sale catalogue described the property as, 'A very substantial Cubitt-built Mansion erected in the year 1865 at a cost of about £50,000, built of white bricks with stone facings and slated and leaded roof. The interior fittings are of a solid and expensive character. The doors to the principal rooms are of oak with panels of burr walnut and maple wood and lined with mahogany. The approach is by a long winding carriage drive protected by two attractive lodges.'

The last occupant of the house was the Marchioness of Ely. One of the lodges mentioned remains today at the north-west junction of Green Dragon Lane and Eversley Crescent, where the two meet Wades Hill. Part of a wall to the Estate can be found at the top of the cul-de-sac Eversley Mount.

The mid 1920s saw Suburban House in Vicars Moor Lane on the market, followed in 1930 by Stone Hall and its Estate, over which The Spinney and Stone Hall Road were built.

In 1929 the Capitol Cinema was opened on the site formerly occupied by Fords Grove Mansion and now occupied by the Capitol House block of offices. It could hold nearly 2,000 people and housed a restaurant, cloakroom and a large car park. Admission prices after 4 p.m., in 1930, were 6d., 9d., 1/3d. and 1/6d. for the Stalls, 1/6d. and 2/- for the Balcony. In 1933 it became part of the A.B.C. chain and it is remembered with some affection by older people.

In 1930 the northwards extension of the Piccadilly line from Finsbury Park was sanctioned. It reached Arnos Grove in 1932 and Cockfosters the following year. Meanwhile, in 1931, the North Circular Road between Silver Street and Palmers Green had been completed. The nearby Huxley farmland along the northern edge of Hedge Lane was sold off between 1930 and 1932, although it was some years before it was entirely built up.

In 1931 what is now the Intimate Theatre was built in Green Lanes as St. Monica's Parish Church Hall. In 1937 it was transformed into a repertory theatre by John Clements and has remained as a theatre, for the main part, until the present time. Amongst the stars who have played there are Vivien Leigh and, in 1949, Roger Moore (then a juvenile).

On 24 September 1931, upon the death of Sir William Paulin, A. Savill & Sons in conjunction with E. J. Westoby, auctioned 36 acres of estate, including Roseneath, Broadfields (20 acres), Rose Cottage and numerous small premises in the district.

The largest lots were purchased by the Ingram family of builders. Arthur, father of George, bought Broadfields and in the mid 1930s built up the modern Broadfields Avenue, Cresswell Way and Paulin Drive, which followed the line of the old coach drive to the mansion. The old mansion stables remain incorporated in the garage on the southern corner with Wades Hill. Next to the garage, in Paulin Drive, is an old circular cottage which used to be Paulin's harness room.

A photograph of Wades Hill prior to the development of the 1930s is shown at Plate 20.

George Ingram bought Roseneath and the playing fields between it and Station Road over which he developed Ringwood Way. He also leased adjoining land off of Radcliffe Road from the Dr. Radcliffe School Estate. He sub leased this land and some of his own Freehold land to Winchmore Hill Bowling Club.

In 1936 the ancient Beaulieu, Firs Lane, was sold for development.

It was, of course, mainly in the inter-War years that Winchmore Hill Wood was built up. It was a slow process begun, as we have seen, as early as 1912. The reason for the slowness appears to have been the piecemeal sale of plots of land by the Taylor family over the years. For example plots along Broad Walk were sold off between 1919 and 1934 (mainly in the 1920s). A major purchaser of these plots was George Ingram, who was also responsible for developing much of Woodland Way.

It is interesting to trace the development of what had been the Wood through a succession of Kelly's Directories, bearing in mind that the roads were often 'laid out' years before houses were built along them and their names entered in the Directories.

Plate 20. A view down Wades Hill, looking north, before this section was developed in the 1930s. The fields belonging to William Paulin of Broadfields are on the left.

None of the roads on the site of the old Wood between Grovelands Park and Hoppers Road appears listed in the 1921 Kelly's. However, the 1922 Directory indicates reasonable habitation of Branscombe Gardens and Seaforth Gardens as well as a few houses along Broad Walk. By the time of the 1927 Directory the first two named of these roads were well developed and several more dwellings had appeared on Broad Walk.

The 1928 Directory marks a further stage of development since Hillfield Park and Woodland Way appear listed for the first time and both have a considerable number of residents. In addition a few houses are now shown along Downes Court. Denleigh Gardens appears in the Directory but has no inhabitants shown!

In 1931 Brackendale makes its debut with a handful of inhabitants indicated. Oaklands and Beechdale also appear listed for the first time and both have a notable number of residents. The 1932 Directory records an increase in inhabited houses along Brackendale.

The 1935 Directory marks the appearance of Woodcroft with a significant number of houses. By this time the number of people living in Broad Walk and Downes Court had also crept up significantly. The Wood had become suburbia.

The inter-War years saw many social changes. It was not uncommon for middle class houses in London to have electricity and the gadgets it served - irons, vacuum cleaners, fires, kettles, etc. This not only led to an increased standard of living for the owner but, also, contributed to a decline in the need for domestic servants so common in this and other areas at the turn of the Century.

By the time the Second World War broke out the modern suburb had been constructed. There was still some infilling to be done between Hedge Lane and Barrowell Green and other small areas but the village of forty years earlier was now only a memory.

CHAPTER TWELVE

1939 Onwards

When War seemed certain the Borough of Southgate set up 38 ARP posts, eventually to be housed in purpose-built constructions with 13½" brick walls and concrete roofs. One of these survived until recently in the Langham Playing Fields. The Headquarters were in the basement of the Town Hall at Palmers Green (now the Library).

In January 1939, at the Government's bequest, a programme of trench shelter building began. Most shelters were lined and covered with concrete or steel. One in Firs Lane had to be pumped to prevent flooding.

Early in 1939 the easily assembled Anderson shelter was available for erection in private grounds. Later on the Council lined them with concrete and fitted them with bunks. The shelters were provided free to those earning less than £350 p.a. There was a legal obligation on employers to provide shelters for their staff and this was often listed as an added amenity in job advertisements.

Parts of London prepared for War by evacuating children but Winchmore Hill, in the outer suburbs, was in what was considered to be a 'safe area' so no arrangements were made.

Britain declared War on Germany on 3 September 1939.

The Baths at Barrowell Green were used as an anti-gas training centre and ambulance post. An Anti-Aircraft battery site was erected in Firs Lane, later to become a Prisoner of War (POW) camp for German soldiers. There was a fire-fighting post by Downes Court, partly funded by private money from local residents. Grovelands became a Red Cross Hospital and the premises of Keble School a First Aid Post. The school itself continued by sharing the facilities of Palmers Green High School, in Hoppers Road, which possessed a strong shelter under the playground.

Naturally there are still a number of people who remember the War time period. One of these is Mr. D. Grammer. He was born in 1925 in Glenwood House and spent most of his life in the district before moving to Harpenden in 1987. He comments,

"In 1942 I was one of the handful of my generation locally who joined the Home Guard. Most of the volunteers were in the 45-55 age range. The 26th Battalion Middlesex Regiment 'D' Company had its HQ at Rowantree House and the commanding officer, later to be my father-in-law, was Major G. R. Nicholson of Houndsden Road. During the winter we paraded about twice a week at St. Paul's Institute but in the summer we would hold outdoor exercises at Worlds End Lane or Langham Playing Fields (as they are now called). I used to keep my .300 rifle at home in a little downstairs cloakroom. At 18 I joined the Royal Marines."

Mr. F. Arnold, who was born in 1933 and moved to Woodberry Avenue in 1940 says, "I recall a V1 ('buzz bomb') hitting the junction of Carpenter Gardens and Highfield Road whilst nearer home a landmine was dropped by parachute onto Langham Playing Fields. For some reason the explosion from this did little to properties in Fernleigh Rd., but blasted out windows in Woodberry Avenue. I also well remember a German plane straffing the top of my road."

Lucy Pettifer says "I remember the Second World War for two of the German POW's. Willy Albrecht of Hamburg and Walter Duchow used to come to Winchmore Hill every day with the German prisoners at Harrow. They demolished Percy Lodge and 'Avondale' and built Barber Close. We found Willy and Walter to be very amiable and entertained them at week-ends and Christmas whenever possible. They obviously appreciated this because after the War, when they had been repatriated, they paid for my husband and me to spend two weeks in Hamburg. Indeed I am still in correspondence with both men and their families."

Towards the end of the War Germany sent a succession of V1 and V2 rockets over the Channel and it is these that appear to have done the most damage in Winchmore Hill. On 7 July 1944 the V1 that Mr. Arnold remembers fell at the junction of Highfield Rd. and Carpenter Gardens. A school, shops and many houses were damaged. Eight people were killed and twenty-four others injured.

In the autumn of 1944 a V1 fell on the AA Searchlight site in

Grovelands Park. There was only minor damage and there were no casualties.

On 29 August 1944 a V1 damaged the hospital at Grovelands to the extent that no further casualty patients could be admitted for a while.

In September 1944 the silent V2 assault started and on 15 November one fell near Ringwood Way and Vicars Moor Lane, demolishing Hood's Cottage and causing other destruction.

In the Borough of Southgate there were about 130 War fatalities and 267 seriously injured. 256 houses were destroyed. As awful as all this was for the families involved it must be remembered that compared to many other parts of London the suburb we are interested in escaped relatively lightly.

The immediate post-War period was marked by rebuilding and austerity. However, one man who remembers the mid 1940s with some warmth is Brian Bennett, drummer with The Shadows and a former pupil of Winchmore Hill School. In 'The Story of The Shadows' compiled by Mike Read, Mr. Bennett, who was born in 1940, is quoted as follows,

'Saturday was the big night out for us: after my face had been scrubbed to make me a cherubic pink colour, and I'd made exaggerated sound effects in the bathroom to give the impression that I was cleaning my teeth, I'd be off to the Capitol Cinema at Winchmore Hill. As with most picture houses in those days, there was a fantastic restaurant where you'd order up expensive-looking cakes, toast and tea cakes and be served by waitresses in smart hats and black and white uniforms. Then with your tummy almost bursting through your blazer buttons, you'd be plunged into the subdued lighting of the cinema, to the strains of an old boy pounding away like the Phantom of the Opera on the theatre organ. They were magic, those nights at Winchmore Hill.'

The Capitol was closed in 1959, to be replaced by the modern Inland Revenue offices.

The reader will recall that Highfield House had been the centre of a large estate in the 19th century and this had mainly been built up in Edwardian times. However, the House itself persisted for some years and during much of the 1920s and 30s was the home of Winchmore Hill High School for Girls. During the War it was used as a Fire Station, but upon conclusion of hostilities it lay vacant and decayed. It was purchased by Southgate Council in 1952 and demolished, to be replaced by the existing Council flats at the junction of Haslemere Road and Arundel Gardens. The latter frontage retains an old Cedar tree that stood in the grounds of the old House.

It is well to remember that although we are talking of the modern era, trolleybuses ran at the time. The 629 travelled from Enfield Town to Tottenham Court Road over a route very similar to the one followed by the present day 29 motor bus. All trolleybuses in the area were withdrawn in 1961.

By the mid 1950s the school adjoining St. Paul's Church had become unsafe and the classes were transferred to the Institute in 1958. The nature of the ground apparently precluded rebuilding on the same site and in June 1958 permission was given to build a new School on the present site in Ringwood Way. On 7 March 1961 it was opened by H.R.H. the Princess Alexandra. A few years later the nearby Institute and the neighbouring curate's house were sold to the Post Office who built their new Sorting Office on the site. The Edwardian premises, on the other corner of Kings Avenue and Station Road, previously used for this purpose, remain in use with a removals company.

In 1965 Southgate, Edmonton and Enfield merged into the London Borough of Enfield as part of a major reorganisation of Local Government within the capital.

Since that time there has been an influx of Cypriots into the area and, more recently, black and Asian faces have been a more common sight locally. These newcomers have been accompanied by numerous caucasians from the mainland of Europe.

In 1977 Enfield Health Authority stopped using Grovelands as a hospital and the building fell into disrepair. By the mid 1980s it was costing about £2,000 p.a. to maintain and more than £30,000 p.a. to secure against intruders. Fortunately a purchaser was found and in September 1986 it reopened as the private psychiatric 'Grovelands Priory Hospital'.

It is interesting to note that as late as 1983 Highlands was still treating 20 patients suffering from Post Encephalitis Lethargica – survivors of an epidemic dating from the Great War period and just after.

Thus we arrive at the modern day and survey a prosperous middle class suburb. What of the quality of life in this era when crime in Britain is spiralling?

I have spoken to numerous older residents and hope to publish their recollections in another book. I do get the feeling that most of the older people preferred life in Winchmore Hill before the last War, when it still retained more of a village feel. However, nearly all the older inhabitants of the area still consider it a pleasant and desirable place to live in. This is quite interesting when one considers the vast changes that have occurred since their youth and the poor publicity often given to the quality of life in modern London.

There are burglaries but these rarely seem to involve violence and there is still, mercifully, little 'street crime'. There are numerous open spaces, including the beautiful Grovelands Park, and public transport is good. There are three bus services along Green Lanes linking with the Piccadilly Line at Wood Green and a frequent British Rail train service into town on the Hertford North line that was electrified in 1976. What of the future?

I have no reason to suppose that life in Winchmore Hill will deteriorate noticeably but I can anticipate that it will lose more of its links with the past and hence its character.

We have noted the passing of Highfield House, The Capitol Cinema and St. Paul's Institute since the War. In addition one may record the replacement of the Victorian Esther Doe Almshouses with the modern ones in 1974. In 1987 Devon House was demolished. There is talk of building on the (now disused) Langham Playing Fields and demolishing Highlands when its proposed merger with Chase Farm Hospital takes place. It is also possible that the New River will fall into disuse soon and the land given over to some other purpose. If these changes do not occur no doubt others will over the years. In the absence of a nuclear holocaust, I can imagine that about 2100 someone will write a book on how things were in 'the old days' when Winchmore Hill boasted an old Quaker Meeting House, a mansion designed by Nash and quaint Edwardian building stock in the Fernleigh Road area. Hopefully Winchmore Hill will still be a pleasant place to live in though.

P.O. London Suburban Directory
Published and Printed by Kelly & Co. 1865
Winchmore Hill

1865 PRIVATE RESIDENTS

Barnes Misses, Laurel Cottage; Bartlett George, Highfield House; Blackall John, Rose Cottage; Bratt Charles; Busk Edward Thos JP, Fords Grove; Condell Henry, The Vale; Cresswell, John; Cresswell, Mrs.; Dawson William Isaac, Model Farm; Feltham John, Roseville; Foster Mr. Charles, Truro Cottage; Frost Rev. John Dixon, BD; Gilbert John Ames, The Firs; Green John, Windermere Villa; Grugeon James Isaac, Crusa Cottage; Harrison Mr. James; Heath Miss, Hope House; Ince Rev. George (Baptist); Kelsey William; Kerne John; Leath James, Winchmore Villa; Lever Charles; Mackney William; Mackreth Henry Wm, Drayton Villa; Mann Thomas, Roseneath House; Marks Rev. John (Independent); Marsh Mr. Edward, Holly Lodge; Morgan Charles jun; Morgan Charles, sen., Moor Park; Morrison Capt. Richard James RN; Naimby Miss, Woodside Cottage; Neville Mr. James; Patten Mr. George; Peacock Mr. Richard; Pollock Mrs., Hoppers Road; Purvis Peregrine Hogg, Cedars; Schofield John, Percy Lodge; Sharp Miss, Chase Side; Simmonds Mr. John, Sutton Lodge; Smith Mrs, Oak Tree Villa; Stride Edward, Man's Lane; Thomas Mrs; Tills Mrs, Fords Grove Cottage; Todd Mrs, Uplands; Vann Mr. John; Villers John Fitzpatrick, Holly Cottage; Wade John, Beaumont Lodge; Whilshin James; Willink Mrs; Wood William, River Cottage.

All the above are designated Esq. in the Directory, unless I have stated otherwise.

COMMERCIAL

Adams Thomas, grocer; Baker Mrs. Maria, haberdasher; Bates John Walker, shopkeeper; Beadle Edmund, upholsterer etc; Beard & King, dressmakers; Binstead William, baker; Bird Miss Elizabeth, dressmaker; Braid George, Florist; Calderwood George, *Green Dragon*; Carpenter Thomas, wheelwright; Childs George (late Udall & Childs), linendraper etc; Clark Thomas, carrier; Cresswell John, surgeon; Critchlow Colin, tailor; Dixon Frederick George, butcher; Eaton John, carrier; Eldridge John Goodison, gardener; Forster William John, carpenter; Fossey John, boot and shoemaker; Frith Anthony, plumber; Goldsworthy Thomas, baker; Gough John, beer retailer; Gurling George, beer retailer; Harlow Alfred, general dealer; Harvey John, farmer, Vale Farm; Harwood Thomas, bootmaker; Hodgson Mrs. Caroline, preparatory school; Humphries John, *Chase Side Tavern*; Hunt Samuel, beer retailer; Hunter David, *Salisbury Arms*; Johnson John, coach painter; Jones John, wheelwright; King John, beer retailer; Langley Mrs. Ann, butcher; Lowing Misses Sophia & Elizbth., shpkeprs; Matthews Francis, *Orange Tree*; Mortiby George, gardener; Newby William, jobmaster; Page James, nurseryman; Palmer Job, *King's Head*; Pomfret James, fruiterer; Riley Mrs. Ann, grocer and Post Office; Sell James, carpenter; Swain William, farmer, Philcap Farm; Watkin Richard, smith; Watkins Miss Mary, day school; Waters James, grocer; Williams William, farmer, The Firs.

APPENDIX 2

Significant Changes from Kelly's 1899-1900 Directory up to World War One

KELLY'S DIRECTORY	ADDITIONS	NAME CHANGES		COMMENTS
		From	To	
1901-02	Arundel Rd.(now Gdns.) Chaseville Park Rd. Elm Park Rd. Haslemere Rd. Station Avenue Wades Grove			Station Avenue later named Roseneath Avenue. No houses along Wades Grove.
1902-03	Orpington Rd.	Chase Side Clapfield Terrace Cock Hill Eversley Rd. Middle Lane Winchmore Hill Rd.	Winchmore Hill Rd. Wilson St. (West Side) Eversley Park Rd. (South) Hounsden Rd. Station Rd. Church Hill	Wades Grove now has ten houses.
1903-04		Highfield Row	Highfield Rd.	
1904-05	'The Broadway' on west of Green Lanes	Hounsden Rd.	Houndsden Rd.	A full range of occupants on 'The Broadway' west side. (None on east.)
1905-06	Cedar Rd. College Rd. Hurst Rd.			Fernleigh Rd. has two houses marked on it.

Year	Streets	Built Up	Notes
			Woodberry Ave. only has 1 occupant. Kings Ave. has 2 houses-occupied by curates, one of whom is Rev. A. J. King (St. Paul's.)
1907-08	Orpington Crescent / River Avenue		Orpington Crescent later renumbered as part of Orpington Road. Woodberry Ave. now houses numerous families. River Avenue developed from its Green Lanes end.
1908-09; 1909-10			Little significant change.
1910-11	Greenwood Gardens / Queens Avenue		No houses along Greenwood Gardens. A Confectioner and Bank now shown on east side of Green Lanes between Holy Trinity Church and Fords Grove.
1911-12		East side of 'The Broadway' Built Up	
1912-13			Little significant change.
1913-14			First houses occupied in Greenwood Gardens.
1914-15			Little significant change.

Note: Oaktree Avenue and Crestbrook Avenue do not appear in pre-World War One Kelly's. The 1914 O.S. map shows them as laid out but they were not built up until post-war.

Bibliography

BOOKS

Armitage, P., Deal, G., Ivens, J., *Excavation of the Roman Settlement, Lincoln Rd., Enfield*, (1977).

Baker, T. F., (ed.) *The Victoria History of the Counties of England. A History of Middlesex*, (1976) Vol. V.

Bath, Tony and Jennifer, *Winchmore Hill Cricket Club. The First Hundred Years 1880-1980*, (1980).

Cecil, David, *The Cecils of Hatfield House*, (1975).

Cresswell, Henrietta, *Memories of a Lost Village*, (1982).

Cresswell, Dr. John, *Dr. Cresswell's Winchmore Hill*.

Croome, D. F., Jackson, A.A., *Rails Through The Clay*, (1962).

Dalling, Graham, *A Guide to Enfield Street Names*, (1982).

Doree, Stephen, *Domesday Book and the Origins of Edmonton Hundred*, (1986).

Edwards, Irene, '1688 Middlesex Village, to Suburb of London, 1938', *Journal of Friends Historical Society*, (1938), p23-39.

Ekwall, E., *The Concise Oxford Dictionary of English Place-Names*, (1936).

Farrant, R. F., *Methodists of Winchmore Hill 1880-1980*, (1980).

Field, J., *Place Names of Greater London*, (1980)

Fisk, Frederick, *The History of The Parish of Edmonton in the County of Middlesex*.

Gillam, Geoffrey, *Enfield at War 1914-18*, (1982).

Gillam, Geoffrey, *Enfield at War 1939-45*, (1985).

Gillam, Geoffrey, *Theatres, Music Halls and Cinemas in the L.B. Enfield*, (1986).

Gover, J. E. B., Mawer, A., Stenton, F. M., *The Place Names of Middlesex*, (1942).

Graham-Campbell, James, *Saxon and Viking Britain*.

Haigh, D., *Old Park in the Manor of Enfield*, (1977).

History of Winchmore Hill Bowling Club 1932-82, (1982).

Hodge, Peter, *Historic Walks in Conservation Areas – Winchmore Hill*, (1973).

Hoy, Denis, *From Fields to Flats – A History of Bush Hill Park and St. Stephen's Church.*

Humphries, S., Weightman, G., *The Making of Modern London 1815-1914*, (1983).

Humphries, S., Weightman, G., *The Making of Modern London 1914-1939*, (1984).

King, Archibald, *A Short History of Winchmore Hill Meeting House and Ground*

Lewis, Tom; Pam, David, *William and Robert Cecil as Landowners in Edmonton and Southgate, 1561-1600 – Two Essays.*

London Transport, *London General, The Story of the London Bus 1856-1956*, (1956).

London Weekend Television, *Into Your Past 1914-39*, (1984).

Lysons, Rev. Daniel, *The Environs of London*, (1795).

Mason, Tom, *A Southgate Scrap-Book*, (1948).

Matthews, P. W., *History of Barclays Bank Limited*, (1926).

Middleton, J., *View of the Agriculture of Middlesex*, (1798).

Morris, John (ed.), *Domesday Book*, (1975)

Newby, H. W., *Old Southgate*, (1949).

Oakleaves, The Local History Bulletin of Southgate Civic Trust, Vol. 1., (1987).

Pam, David, *The Fight for Common Rights in Enfield and Edmonton 1400-1600*, (1973).

Pam, David, *The New Enfield. Stories of Enfield, Edmonton and Southgate*, (1977).

Pam, David, *The Hungry Years, The Struggle for Survival in Edmonton and Enfield before 1400*, (1980).

Pam, David, *Southgate and Winchmore Hill, A Short History*, (1982).

Pam, David, *The Story of Enfield Chase* (1984).

Pugh, R. B., *The Victoria History of The Counties of England. A History of Middlesex*, (1969), Vol. 1.

Read, Mike, *The Story of The Shadows.*

Regnart, Horace, *Memories of Winchmore Hill*, (1952).

Rickson, T. John, 'The Edmonton Enclosure 1801-2' *Middlesex Local History Council Bulletin*, No. 13. (March 1962), pp12-15 (inc.).

Robbins, Michael, *A New Survey of England: Middlesex*, (1953).

Roberts, E. M., *History of Palmers Green High School.*

Robinson, William, *The History and Antiquities of Edmonton in The County of Middlesex*, (1819).

Round, Walker, *The Story of Southgate and Winchmore Hill*, (1906).

Smith, John Thomas, *A Book For a Rainy Day or Recollection of the Events of the Years 1766-1833*, (1905).

Smith, Stevie, *Me Again*, (1981).

Southgate Civic Trust, *Walks in Southgate and Winchmore Hill*, (1978).

Southgate District Handbook and Ratepayers' Guide, (1909).

Spalding, Eric W., *Looking Outward – The Story of St. Paul's , Winchmore Hill Parish Church*, (1966)

St. Monica's Church, *1910-1985*, (1985).

The Book of Middlesex, (1930).

Thames Water, *History of the New River.*

Thorne, James, *Handbook to the Environs of London*, (1983).

Walford, Edward, *Village London*, Part 2, (1985).

Welldon Finn, R., *Domesday Book – A Guide*, (1986).

Whitaker, C. W., *History of Enfield*, (1969).

Winchmore Hill United Reformed Church, *Handbook for 1987-8*, (1987).

NEWSPAPERS

The Southgate Messenger and General Advertiser (September 1856 - August 1857).

The North Middlesex and Southgate Messenger (September 1857 - December 1862).

Tottenham and Edmonton Weekly Herald (July - October 1869; April 1874 - July 1875).

Winchmore Hill Journal, Vol. 1, No. 9, (1903).

Recorder for Palmers Green, Winchmore Hill and Southgate (1907-16) Vols. 1-9 (inc.).

Palmers Green and Southgate Gazette, (1915/16; January 1920 - October 1922; 2 January 1931).

The Gazette (6 September 1984).

Enfield Advertiser (14 November 1985).

DIRECTORIES, FACT SHEETS AND PARLIAMENTARY PROCEEDINGS

Various Directories produced by Kelly, Pigot and Robson.

Fact Sheets on Population; Railways and Tramways & Trolleybuses produced by L. B. Enfield Local History Unit.

Commons and Lords Proceedings for The Edmonton Local Board (Division of District) Act 1881.

CATALOGUES AND PROGRAMMES

Catalogue for the sale of 'The Grove' Estate, 1834.

Catalogue for the sale of Eaton Park Rd. land, 26 July 1893.

Catalogue for the sale of the Taylor Estates, 9 June 1902.

Catalogue for the sale of Grovelands, 1919.

Southgate U.D.C., *Programme for Opening of Grovelands Park, 12 April 1913.*

MAPS

Ordnance Survey Maps (or reduced reproductions) as follows –

– Map of Britain in the Dark Ages at 1 inch to 16 miles, (1974).

– Winchmore Hill in 1865 at 25 inches to the mile.

– Winchmore Hill in 1895 at 25 inches to the mile.

– Barnet and Southgate in 1895 at six inches to the mile (Published 1897).

– Barnet and Southgate in 1912 at six inches to the mile. (Published 1920.)

PRIVATE PAPERS, PHOTOGRAPHS, MAPS, ETC.

A number of the individuals and Institutions listed in the Acknowledgements Section have kindly allowed me sight of various unpublished papers on the area. These are too numerous to list here.

Index